THANKSGIVING RECIPES

Plant-based Recipes to Celebrate the Holidays

(Delicious Thanksgiving Family Recipes)

Kyle McElyea

Published by Alex Howard

© Kyle McElyea

All Rights Reserved

Thanksgiving Recipes: Plant-based Recipes to Celebrate the Holidays (Delicious Thanksgiving Family Recipes)

ISBN 978-1-989891-91-9

All rights reserved. No part of this guide may be reproduced in any form without permission in writing from the publisher except in the case of brief quotations embodied in critical articles or reviews.

Legal & Disclaimer

The information contained in this book is not designed to replace or take the place of any form of medicine or professional medical advice. The information in this book has been provided for educational and entertainment purposes only.

The information contained in this book has been compiled from sources deemed reliable, and it is accurate to the best of the Author's knowledge; however, the Author cannot guarantee its accuracy and validity and cannot be held liable for any errors or omissions. Changes are periodically made to this book. You must consult your doctor or get professional medical advice before using any of the suggested remedies, techniques, or information in this book.

Table of contents

Part 1 1
Introduction 2
Chapter 1: Thanksgiving Appetizers 3
Artichoke Hearts Gratin 3
Bacon Stuffed Mushrooms 5
Bacon Wrapped Green Beans 8
Baked Brie with Maple Caramelized Apples and Spiced Praline Bacon 10
Baked Chestnuts 12
Baked Cranberry Jalapeno Dip 14
Baked Stuffed Brie with Cranberries Walnuts 16
Best Pickled Eggs in all of Ottawa 18
Best Spinach Dip Ever 20
Blue Cheese and Pear Tartlets 22
Brie Cheese Pizza 24
Buttermilk Corn Fritters 25
Caprese Appetizer 27
Caramel Snack Mix 28
Cheese Ball 30
Cheese Fondue 31
Cheesy Spinach Squares 32
Chef Johns Hot Spinach Artichoke Dip 33
Chocolate Chip Cheese Ball 35
Classic Savory Deviled Eggs 37
Corn Fritters 39

- Country French Cheese ... 41
- Crab Stuffed Mushrooms ... 43
- Cranberry Brie Bites ... 45
- Cranberry Dip ... 47
- Cranberry Jalapeno Cream Cheese Dip ... 49
- Cranberry Meatballs ... 51
- Cranberry Relish Pizza ... 53
- Cranberry Salsa ... 55
- Cream Cheese Ball ... 56
- Cream Cheese Penguins ... 57
- Crispy Rosemary Sea Salt Flatbread Crackers ... 59
- DeepFried Stuffing ... 61
- Deviled Eggs ... 63
- Deviled Eggs I ... 65
- Dried Fruit Cheese Ball ... 66
- Easy Awesome Shrimp Scampi ... 67
- Easy Baked Brie with Almonds and Brown Sugar ... 68
- Easy Pumpkin Dip ... 70
- Festive Cheese Dip Slaw ... 71
- Festive Cracker Spread ... 73
- Feta Cheese Foldovers ... 74
- Fluffy Fruit Dip ... 76
- Fruit Dip ... 77
- Glazed Nuts ... 78
- Grammies Cranberry Salsa ... 80
- Grandmas Stuffed Celery ... 81
- Grilled Oysters with Fennel Butter ... 83

Heavenly Shrimp Dip	85
Herman Reunion Cheese Ball	86
Holiday Crabmeat Ball	88
Hot Artichoke and Spinach Dip II	90
Hot Artichoke Dip	92
Hot Crab Dip	93
Hot Spinach Red Pepper Dip	94
Jalapeno Popper Cups	96
Jamies Baked Brie	97
Kosher Pineapple Cranberry Salsa Pareve	99
Kristas Queso	101
Microwave Spiced Nuts	102
Momma Hallmarks Cheese Balls	103
Mouth Watering Stuffed Mushrooms	104
Olive Puffs	106
Parmesan and Parsley Sausage Ball Appetizer	107
Parmesan Baskets	108
Pecan Snack	110
Peppered Pecans	111
Perfect Deviled Eggs	113
Pickled Eggs III	115
Pine Cone Cheese Ball	117
Pumpkin Dip	119
Pumpkin Peanut Dip	120
RanchStyle Deviled Eggs	121
Rosemary and Brown Sugar Mixed Nuts	122
Rosemary Sage Squash Seeds	124

Sausage Stuffed Mushrooms 126

Sausage Stuffing Balls 128

Savory Pumpkin Hummus 130

Seasoned Crackers 132

Serious Herb Cheese Spread 133

Shrimp Cheese Ball 135

Shrimp Dip 137

Simple Deviled Eggs 138

Part 2 140

Introduction 141

Cider roasted chicken 142

Smoky pumpkin beer and potato soup 144

Harvest cranberry, burrata salad 147

Skilallow cranberry roasted 148

Crockpot beef chili 150

Fall harvest quinoa salad 152

Thanksgiving turkey hot dish 154

Roasted butternut persimmon salad 155

Pumpkin butter rugelach cookies 158

Caramelized garlic butter 160

Butternut squash 162

Roasted squash, caramelized fig 164

Brie stuffed crispy 166

Cinnamon streemployl 167

Tomato white lasagna 169

Pistachio chocolate baklava 171

Cheesy hasselback potato 174

Roasted lemon spinach 175

Cheese-maker mac and cheese.. 177

Cinnamon spiced dutch with cranberry butter........................... 179

Cheddar apple butternut squash soup 181

Butternut squash cheese ravioli 183

6 ingredient spiced pumpkin butter... 185

Potato rolls.. 187

Bourbon casserole.. 189

Part 1

Introduction

What could be more exciting than Thanksgiving Holiday?

No doubt about it. Each time a holiday like Thanksgiving or Christmas draws near, I just couldn't help feeling so pumped up. Something about the traditions, family get-togethers, and reliving fond childhood memories (and creating new ones) conjure a warm, fuzzy feeling. Holidays are truly special and amazing. They never fail to put a smile on my face.

The best thing about the holidays? They get me excited to cook!

In the cookbook series of holidays and events, we celebrate the lip-smacking, delicious recipes served during different festivities for the whole year—from the New Year's Day, Easter, and Halloween to Thanksgiving, Christmas, and New Year's Eve. This series has a chock-full of recipes that will surely make your holidays both unforgettably delicious and deliciously unforgettable! You are handling the book "Halloween Cookbook 365 Volume 1"

This series, we cover a wide range of holidays in detail: starting from the New Year's Day up until the New Year's Eve, and everything in between. Welcome the New Year with a wonderful cocktail party, prepare something romantic for your sweetheart at Valentine's dinner, give mom a special breakfast in bed for Mother's Day, or throw a party for the Big Game for your football-enthusiast friends. You'll definitely find the perfect recipe for any occasion in this book. There are so many possibilities for delicious holiday treats.

Chapter 1: Thanksgiving Appetizers

Artichoke Hearts Gratin

"This easy, all-veggie appetizer idea is proof you don't have to make a dish, to reinvent it."

Serving: 4 | Prep: 10 m | Cook: 10 m | Ready in: 35 m

Ingredients

- 6 canned artichoke hearts, drained and halved
- 1 teaspoon vegetable oil
- salt and freshly ground black pepper to taste
- 2 tablespoons dry b
- read crumbs
- 1/4 cup finely grated Parmigiano-Reggiano cheese
- 1 tablespoon olive oil
- 1/2 lemon, cut into wedges

Direction

- Place artichoke heart halves on a paper towel cut-side down to drain for about 15 minutes.
- Set oven rack about 6 inches from the heat source and preheat the oven's broiler. Line a baking sheet with aluminum foil and lightly coat with vegetable oil.
- Place artichoke heart halves on the prepared baking sheet, cut side up. Season with salt and pepper, sprinkle with breadcrumbs and Parmigiano-Reggiano cheese, and drizzle with olive oil.
- Broil artichoke hearts until browned on top, about 7 minutes. Serve with lemon wedges.

Nutrition Information

- Calories: 89 calories
- Total Fat: 6.2 g
- Cholesterol: 4 mg
- Sodium: 268 mg
- Total Carbohydrate: 6.3 g
- Protein: 3.3 g

Bacon Stuffed Mushrooms

"The melted cheese and bacon make these irresistible! These mushrooms are simple and delicious! Add some of your diced favorites! Omit bacon for vegetarian version."

Serving: 6 | Prep: 20 m | Cook: 30 m | Ready in: 50 m

Ingredients

- 4 slices bacon
- 2 (12 ounce) packages fresh white mushrooms
- 3 tablespoons butter, melted
- 6 pitted black olives, finely chopped
- 1/4 cup finely chopped green onion
- 1 teaspoon oil-packed minced garlic
- 1/2 teaspoon salt
- 1/4 teaspoon ground black pepper
- 1 pinch cayenne pepper
- 1 tablespoon all-purpose flour
- 1/4 cup milk

- 4 slices Swiss-flavored American cheese, chopped
- 3 tablespoons grated Parmesan cheese

Direction

- Preheat oven to 375 degrees F (190 degrees C).
- Place bacon in a large skillet and cook over medium-high heat, turning occasionally, until evenly browned, about 10 minutes. Transfer bacon slices to paper towels, reserving bacon drippings in the skillet. Crumble bacon when cooled.
- Remove stems from mushrooms and set stems aside. Place mushrooms, hollow sides up, on a baking sheet; brush the insides with melted butter.
- Chop mushroom stems; cook and stir chopped stems, black olives, green onion, and crumbled bacon in the bacon drippings over medium heat until mushroom stems release their liquid, about 5 minutes. Add garlic, salt, black pepper, and cayenne pepper; stir to coat.
- Tilt the skillet slightly; move vegetable-bacon mixture to one side, allowing the bacon drippings to pool to the other side. Whisk flour into bacon drippings until smooth and paste-like; slowly stir in milk until gravy is smooth. Mix vegetable-bacon mixture into the gravy. Add American cheese and Parmesan cheese; cook and stir until cheeses melt, about 5 minutes. Spoon filling into mushroom caps.
- Bake in the preheated oven until mushrooms are tender and filling is lightly browned, about 20 minutes. Remove mushrooms from baking sheet and cool on platter for 2 minutes before serving.

Nutrition Information

- Calories: 258 calories
- Total Fat: 22.1 g
- Cholesterol: 48 mg
- Sodium: 770 mg

- Total Carbohydrate: 7.1 g
- Protein: 11.4 g

Bacon Wrapped Green Beans

"Bacon wrapped green beans sprinkled with a little brown sugar, salt and pepper and popped in the oven turn plain green beans into something guest will love and kids can't help but gobble up."

Serving: 8 | Prep: 15 m | Cook: 20 m | Ready in: 35 m

Ingredients

- 1 (12 ounce) package bacon, strips cut in half
- 1 (16 ounce) package frozen cut green beans
- 2 tablespoons brown sugar
- salt and pepper to taste

Direction

- Preheat oven to 350 degrees F (175 degrees C). Grease a casserole dish.
- Set out the bacon, green beans and casserole dish in a little assembly line. Lay out a half strip of bacon. Place a small bunch of green beans (6 or 7) onto the strip of bacon and roll

up into a bundle. Place the bundle into the casserole dish, seam side down. Repeat with remaining bacon strips and green beans. You can pack these pretty tight in the pan, just know that if the bacon is touching another bundle they take some prying to get apart. Sprinkle with the brown sugar and salt and pepper.
- Bake in the preheated oven until browned and heated through, about 20 minutes.

Nutrition Information

- Calories: 226 calories
- Total Fat: 19.2 g
- Cholesterol: 29 mg
- Sodium: 355 mg
- Total Carbohydrate: 7.2 g
- Protein: 5.7 g

Baked Brie with Maple Caramelized Apples and Spiced Praline Bacon

"This is a party in your mouth. Creamy, smoky, spicy, sweet, this recipe makes for a dramatic appetizer that will wow at your Thanksgiving cocktail hour! The recipe also works with a 16-ounce round of Brie if you're feeding a big crowd. Serve with a baguette or your favorite crackers."

Serving: 8 | Prep: 25 m | Cook: 8 m | Ready in: 33 m

Ingredients

- 3 slices bacon
- 2 tablespoons finely chopped pecans
- 1 tablespoon brown sugar
- 1 teaspoon chili powder
- sea salt to taste
- 2 tablespoons unsalted butter
- 2 Golden Delicious apples - peeled, cored, and cut into 1/2-inch thick slices
- 3 tablespoons pure maple syrup
- 1/4 teaspoon ground cinnamon
- 1 (8 ounce) round Brie cheese
- 1 teaspoon chopped fresh rosemary (optional)

Direction

- Preheat oven to 350 degrees F (175 degrees C). Line a baking sheet with aluminum foil.
- Lay bacon on the prepared baking sheet. Mix pecans, brown sugar, chili powder, and sea salt together in a bowl. Sprinkle evenly over the bacon.

- Bake in the preheated oven until crisp, and browned, 18 to 20 minutes. Transfer to a rack to cool. Chop bacon into rough pieces.
- Melt butter in a nonstick skillet over medium-high heat. Add apples and 1 tablespoon maple syrup. Sauté, stirring only every 60 to 90 seconds, until apples are tender and brown, about 8 minutes. Mix in remaining 2 tablespoons maple syrup and cinnamon. Transfer to a bowl.
- Cut a round of parchment paper slightly larger than the round of Brie cheese. Place the Brie cheese on the parchment paper; place onto a baking sheet. Top with the cooked apples to make a big mound.
- Bake in the hot oven for 5 minutes. Add bacon-praline mixture on top of the Brie. Continue baking until top is bubbly, 2 to 3 minutes more. Transfer to a serving platter using a large spatula. Sprinkle with sea salt and rosemary.

Nutrition Information

- Calories: 193 calories
- Total Fat: 13.5 g
- Cholesterol: 40 mg
- Sodium: 302 mg
- Total Carbohydrate: 11.6 g
- Protein: 7.5 g

Baked Chestnuts

"My Grandmother made these delicious chestnuts every Christmas, and they are a real treat!"

Serving: 8 | Prep: 15 m | Cook: 20 m | Ready in: 8 h 50 m

Ingredients

- 1/4 cup ketchup
- 2 tablespoons soy sauce
- 1 1/2 tablespoons vinegar
- 1 pinch ground black pepper
- 1 pinch garlic powder
- 16 canned or jarred whole chestnuts
- 8 slices bacon, cut in half crosswise
- 1/2 cup brown sugar

Direction

- Place the ketchup, soy sauce, vinegar, black pepper, and garlic powder in a resealable plastic bag, and add the chestnuts. Squeeze the bag several times to mix the ingredients, and squeeze air out of the bag. Seal the bag, and marinate the chestnuts overnight.
- The next day, preheat oven to 400 degrees F (205 degrees C). Line a baking sheet with parchment paper.
- Remove chestnuts from the marinade, and shake off excess marinade. Wrap each chestnut in half a bacon slice, and secure with a toothpick. Place brown sugar into a shallow bowl, and roll each wrapped chestnut in brown sugar. Place the appetizers onto the prepared baking sheet.

- Bake chestnuts in the preheated oven until the bacon is crisp and the brown sugar is bubbling, about 20 minutes. Allow to cool before serving.

Nutrition Information

- Calories: 156 calories
- Total Fat: 4.2 g
- Cholesterol: 10 mg
- Sodium: 524 mg
- Total Carbohydrate: 25.5 g
- Protein: 4.4 g

Baked Cranberry Jalapeno Dip

"Tart and spicy, this baked cheese dip will liven up any gathering."

Serving: 40 | Prep: 10 m | Ready in: 40 m

Ingredients

- 10 slices LAND O LAKES® Deli American, cut into 1/4-inch pieces
- 1 (8 ounce) package cream cheese, softened
- 2 tablespoons jarred jalapeno pepper, chopped
- 2 cups frozen cranberries
- 2 tablespoons sugar
- Baguette slices, toasted (optional)

Direction

- Heat oven to 350 degrees F.
- Combine cheeses and jalapenos in bowl; mix well.
- Place cranberries and sugar in another bowl; toss to coat. Gently stir cranberries into cheese mixture.
- Spread mixture into 1-quart casserole dish. Bake 30-35 minutes or until bubbly around edges.
- Serve with baguette slices, if desired.

Nutrition Information

- Calories: 46 calories
- Total Fat: 3.7 g
- Cholesterol: 11 mg
- Sodium: 98 mg
- Total Carbohydrate: 1.9 g

- Protein: 1.4 g

Baked Stuffed Brie with Cranberries Walnuts

"One of the most common mistakes people make when serving cheese is not letting it come to room temperature first, so that all the flavors can be fully realized. This beautiful baked stuffed brie takes that principle to the next level."

Serving: 8 | Prep: 20 m | Ready in: 1 h 40 m

Ingredients

- 1 small wheel of brie (about 6 to 8 inches), chilled
- 1/4 cup dried cranberries
- 1/4 cup chopped walnuts
- 1 sheet frozen puff pastry, thawed, plus extra for (optional) design
- 1 egg, beaten with
- 1 teaspoon water

Direction

- Score the side of a wheel of brie all the way around with a sharp paring knife. Cut directly on the "equator" through the rind. Using a long piece of string or dental floss, wrap the string around the brie on the newly made cut. Loop one end of the string over the other (a half knot). Then pulling the ends of the string in opposite directions, cut the brie in half.
- Press the dried cranberries on one cut side of the brie, and the walnuts on the other. Quickly put the 2 sides back together with the cranberries on top of the walnuts. Press together and stuff back in any cranberries or walnuts that fell out.
- Roll out a thawed sheet of puff pastry on a floured surface to about 1/8-inch thickness. Place brie in center of pastry.

Gently pull up edges to ensure you have enough dough to entirely wrap the brie. You can trim off the corners if there is too much dough. Brush the dough with the egg wash. Fold one edge of the dough over the brie and then the opposite side. Fold over the remaining edges and complexly encase the brie. You can trim off excess pieces of dough, if necessary. Flip the brie over so the seam is at the bottom; gently press in the sides to snug the dough against the brie. Brush the top and sides of the wrapped brie with egg wash.

- If you choose to decorate the brie with cut-out shapes of additional puff pastry, use very cold (almost still frozen) dough to ensure sharp lines. Lightly brush the decorative pieces with egg wash. Place the brie in the freezer for one hour (this is a crucial step; see note below).
- Preheat oven to 425 degrees F (220 degrees C). Line a rimmed baking sheet with parchment paper.
- Place the brie on the prepared baking sheet. Bake on the center rack in preheated oven until it is browned and leaking cheese, about 20 minutes. (Only rarely does the brie not leak through, but 20 to 25 minutes is about how long it takes to melt the cheese and brown the pastry.)

Nutrition Information

- Calories: 304 calories
- Total Fat: 22.3 g
- Cholesterol: 49 mg
- Sodium: 261 mg
- Total Carbohydrate: 17.4 g
- Protein: 9.3 g

Best Pickled Eggs in all of Ottawa

"This is a nice and easy recipe, however it requires using a couple preserving jars."

Serving: 12

Ingredients

- 12 eggs
- 4 cups distilled white vinegar
- 6 cloves garlic
- 1 tablespoon whole white peppercorns
- 1 tablespoon whole allspice
- 2 slices fresh ginger root (optional)

Direction

- Place eggs in saucepan and cover with water. Bring to boil. Cover, remove from heat, and let eggs sit in hot water for 10 to 12 minutes. Cool in cold water and peel.
- In a saucepan, combine vinegar, garlic, peppercorns and allspice. Add sliced ginger if desired. Simmer for 10 minutes.
- Place eggs in sterilized preserving jars. Pour vinegar mixture over eggs; strain if desired.
- Seal and immerse jars in preserving saucepan with rack to hold jars at least 1-inch water above tops of jars. Cover and boil for 10 minutes. Remove jars and cool. Check seals, the lid should not move at all when pressed. Store about one month before opening.

Nutrition Information

- Calories: 79 calories

- Total Fat: 5 g
- Cholesterol: 186 mg
- Sodium: 71 mg
- Total Carbohydrate: 1.7 g
- Protein: 6.5 g

Best Spinach Dip Ever

"This is my dad's recipe. The entire family loves it! A flavorful spinach mixture fills a tasty bread bowl. Your family will love it, too."

Serving: 6 | Prep: 15 m | Ready in: 6 h 15 m

Ingredients

- 1 cup mayonnaise
- 1 (16 ounce) container sour cream
- 1 (1.8 ounce) package dry leek soup mix
- 1 (4 ounce) can water chestnuts, drained and chopped
- 1/2 (10 ounce) package frozen chopped spinach, thawed and drained
- 1 (1 pound) loaf round sourdough bread

Direction

- In a medium bowl, mix together mayonnaise, sour cream, dry leek soup mix, water chestnuts and chopped spinach. Chill in the refrigerator 6 hours, or overnight.
- Watch Now
- Remove top and interior of sourdough bread. Fill with mayonnaise mixture. Tear removed bread chunks into pieces for dipping.
- Watch Now

Nutrition Information

- Calories: 682 calories
- Total Fat: 47.4 g
- Cholesterol: 48 mg

- Sodium: 1183 mg
- Total Carbohydrate: 53.2 g
- Protein: 13.3 g

Blue Cheese and Pear Tartlets

"Tasty, hot appetizers that take little time to prepare but will impress your guests!"

Serving: 15 | Prep: 10 m | Cook: 25 m | Ready in: 35 m

Ingredients

- 4 ounces blue cheese, crumbled
- 1 ripe pear - peeled, cored, and chopped
- 2 tablespoons light cream
- ground black pepper to taste
- 1 (2.1 ounce) package mini phyllo tart shells

Direction

- Pre-bake phyllo shells according to package directions. Set aside to cool.
- Mix together blue cheese, pear, and cream. Season to taste with pepper. Spoon mixture into cooled shells.
- Bake at 350 degrees F (175 degrees C) for 15 minutes. Serve warm.

Nutrition Information

- Calories: 60 calories
- Total Fat: 3.6 g
- Cholesterol: 7 mg
- Sodium: 116 mg
- Total Carbohydrate: 4.5 g
- Protein: 2.2 g

Brie Cheese Pizza

"This is a great appetizer that tastes great and takes seconds to prepare! Just layer Brie cheese and almonds on a pre-made pizza crust, and bake!"

Serving: 16 | Prep: 10 m | Cook: 10 m | Ready in: 20 m

Ingredients

- 8 1/2 ounces Brie cheese, thinly sliced
- 2 cups sliced almonds
- 1 (14 ounce) package purchased fully baked pizza crust (such as Boboli®)

Direction

- Preheat an oven to 350 degrees F (175 degrees C).
- Arrange Brie slices on pizza crust; cover with sliced almonds. Bake until cheese is melted and almonds are toasted, about 10 minutes. Slice into small wedges to serve.

Nutrition Information

- Calories: 228 calories
- Total Fat: 14.7 g
- Cholesterol: 18 mg
- Sodium: 240 mg
- Total Carbohydrate: 16.1 g
- Protein: 10.4 g

Buttermilk Corn Fritters

"Quick and easy corn fritters. Serve with maple syrup or molasses."

Serving: 16

Ingredients

- 1 1/3 cups buttermilk baking mix
- 1 1/2 teaspoons baking powder
- 1 (14.75 ounce) can cream-style corn
- 1 egg, beaten
- 1 cup vegetable oil
- 1 1/2 cups maple syrup

Direction

- In a medium mixing bowl, sift together baking mix and baking powder. In a small mixing bowl, combine corn and egg.
- Combine egg and flour mixture, stir gently.
- Heat oil in large skillet over medium heat. Drop batter by tablespoonfuls into hot oil one layer at a time. Fry for 2 minutes on each side or until golden brown. Drain fritters on absorbent paper. Serve immediately with maple syrup or molasses.

Nutrition Information

- Calories: 255 calories
- Total Fat: 14.4 g
- Cholesterol: 12 mg
- Sodium: 319 mg

- Total Carbohydrate: 31.9 g
- Protein: 1.7 g

Caprese Appetizer

"Caprese salad skewers. Perfect for holiday parties."

Serving: 10 | Prep: 15 m | Ready in: 15 m

Ingredients

- 20 grape tomatoes
- 10 ounces mozzarella cheese, cubed
- 2 tablespoons extra virgin olive oil
- 2 tablespoons fresh basil leaves, chopped
- 1 pinch salt
- 1 pinch ground black pepper
- 20 toothpicks

Direction

- Toss tomatoes, mozzarella cheese, olive oil, basil, salt, and pepper together in a bowl until well coated. Skewer one tomato and one piece of mozzarella cheese on each toothpick.

Nutrition Information

- Calories: 104 calories
- Total Fat: 7.3 g
- Cholesterol: 18 mg
- Sodium: 179 mg
- Total Carbohydrate: 2.4 g
- Protein: 7.2 g

Caramel Snack Mix

"This is the most requested item I bring to the office. It has become the Christmas gift of choice from my kitchen."

Serving: 20 | Prep: 10 m | Cook: 1 h | Ready in: 1 h 10 m

Ingredients

- 1/2 cup butter
- 3/4 cup white corn syrup
- 1 cup packed brown sugar
- 1 cup chopped pecans
- 1 cup almonds
- 1 (12 ounce) package crispy corn and rice cereal

Direction

- Preheat oven to 275 degrees F (135 degrees C). Spray a large roasting pan with non-stick cooking spray.
- In a medium-size microwave safe bowl, mix butter, white corn syrup and brown sugar. Place the mixture in the microwave and cook 2 minutes, or until butter melts.
- Place the cereal, pecans and almonds into the prepared roasting pan. Pour the melted butter mixture over the cereal and nuts and mix gently until the cereal and nuts are coated.
- Bake for 1 hour, stirring every 15 minutes.
- As the snack mix is cooling, be sure to continue to stir so that the mix will not harden in one big lump.

Nutrition Information

- Calories: 262 calories

- Total Fat: 12.6 g
- Cholesterol: 12 mg
- Sodium: 183 mg
- Total Carbohydrate: 36.9 g
- Protein: 3.4 g

Cheese Ball

"This is a great appetizer with a cheesy yet sweet flavor."

Serving: 20 | Prep: 5 m | Cook: 10 m | Ready in: 15 m

Ingredients

- 2 (8 ounce) packages cream cheese
- 1 (8 ounce) can crushed pineapple, drained
- 1 tablespoon diced onion
- 1 tablespoon chopped green bell pepper
- 1/4 tablespoon seasoning salt
- 1 cup chopped pecans

Direction

- Mix together the cream cheese, pineapple, onion, bell pepper and seasoning salt.
- Form into a ball and roll in chopped pecans. Chill and serve with butter crackers.

Nutrition Information

- Calories: 123 calories
- Total Fat: 11.7 g
- Cholesterol: 25 mg
- Sodium: 101 mg
- Total Carbohydrate: 3.2 g
- Protein: 2.3 g

Cheese Fondue

"I've been making this fondue since the early 70's. Always so good!"

Serving: 5

Ingredients

- 1 cup dry white wine
- 1/2 pound shredded Swiss cheese
- 1/2 pound shredded Gruyere cheese
- 2 tablespoons all-purpose flour
- 1/4 teaspoon salt
- 1/4 teaspoon ground nutmeg
- 1 (1 pound) loaf French bread, cut into 1 inch cubes

Direction

- Simmer wine in fondue pot. Add Swiss cheese, Gruyere cheese, 1/4 pound at a time. Stir after each addition of cheese until melted. Stir in flour. When all the cheese has melted, stir in salt and nutmeg. Serve with cut-up French bread.

Nutrition Information

- Calories: 670 calories
- Total Fat: 28.9 g
- Cholesterol: 91 mg
- Sodium: 940 mg
- Total Carbohydrate: 56.9 g
- Protein: 36.5 g

Cheesy Spinach Squares

"My mother used to make these for Thanksgiving and Christmas. They are easy to make and is great for holiday meals. You will love this recipe even if you don't like spinach!"

Serving: 12 | Prep: 5 m | Cook: 50 m | Ready in: 1 h

Ingredients

- 5 (10 ounce) packages frozen chopped spinach
- 1/2 cup butter
- 1 onion, chopped
- 2 cups milk
- 2 cups grated Cheddar cheese
- 1/4 cup all-purpose flour
- 1/4 teaspoon ground black pepper
- 3 eggs, beaten

Direction

- Preheat oven to 350 degrees F (175 degrees C). Grease one 9x13-inch baking dish.
- Bring a large pot of water to a boil and add spinach. Cover, reduce heat, and cook until heated through, 5 to 6 minutes. Drain well, squeezing out excess moisture with your hands. Set aside to cool.
- Melt butter in a saucepan over medium heat; stir in onion and cook until soft and translucent, 5 to 10 minutes.
- Transfer onions to a double boiler; mix in milk, Cheddar cheese, flour, and ground black pepper; cook and stir until blended and smooth, about 5 minutes. Remove from heat; fold in eggs and spinach. Pour the spinach mixture into baking dish and smooth top.

- Bake, uncovered, in the preheated oven until a toothpick inserted in the center comes out clean, about 30 minutes. Cool briefly before cutting into squares.

Nutrition Information

- Calories: 233 calories
- Total Fat: 16.7 g
- Cholesterol: 90 mg
- Sodium: 294 mg
- Total Carbohydrate: 11 g
- Protein: 12.5 g

Chef Johns Hot Spinach Artichoke Dip

"I've always enjoyed hot spinach artichoke dip, but it always struck me as a little oily.
I decided to try a mayo-less version, and then raised the stakes even higher by excluding the sour cream as well. To counter this, a bit more cheese was added, and the results were amazing. A rich, creamy, cheesy, not greasy dip."

Serving: 6 | Prep: 15 m | Cook: 30 m | Ready in: 45 m

Ingredients

- 2 tablespoons butter
- 1/2 cup green onions, white and light green parts only, thinly sliced
- 2 cloves garlic, minced
- salt
- 1 (14 ounce) can artichoke hearts, drained and chopped

- 1 (10 ounce) package frozen chopped spinach, thawed, drained and squeezed dry
- 8 ounces cream cheese
- 1/2 cup shredded Gruyere cheese
- 1/2 cup finely grated Parmigiano-Reggiano cheese
- 1/4 teaspoon hot sauce
- 1 pinch ground nutmeg
- salt and freshly ground black pepper to taste
- 1/4 cup shredded mozzarella cheese

Direction

- Preheat oven to 400 degrees F (200 degrees C).
- Melt butter in a saucepan over medium-low heat; stir in onions and pinch of salt. Cook, stirring occasionally, until onions are soft, about 5 minutes. Stir garlic into onions and remove from heat.
- Mix green onion mixture, spinach, artichoke hearts, cream cheese, Gruyere, Parmigiano-Reggiano, hot sauce, nutmeg, salt, and pepper in a large bowl until combined.
- Spoon artichoke mixture into two ramekins. Top each with shredded mozzarella cheese.
- Bake in the preheated oven until tops are golden brown and bubbling, about 25 minutes.

Nutrition Information

- Calories: 284 calories
- Total Fat: 22.9 g
- Cholesterol: 71 mg
- Sodium: 637 mg
- Total Carbohydrate: 8.8 g
- Protein: 12.7 g

Chocolate Chip Cheese Ball

"A sweet switch from the usual cheese ball. Serve with graham crackers or chocolate wafers."

Serving: 32 | Prep: 20 m | Ready in: 3 h 20 m

Ingredients

- 1 (8 ounce) package cream cheese, softened
- 1/2 cup butter, softened
- 3/4 cup confectioners' sugar
- 2 tablespoons brown sugar
- 1/4 teaspoon vanilla extract
- 3/4 cup miniature semisweet chocolate chips
- 3/4 cup finely chopped pecans

Direction

- In a medium bowl, beat together cream cheese and butter until smooth. Mix in confectioners' sugar, brown sugar and vanilla. Stir in chocolate chips. Cover, and chill in the refrigerator for 2 hours.
- Shape chilled cream cheese mixture into a ball. Wrap with plastic, and chill in the refrigerator for 1 hour.
- Roll the cheese ball in finely chopped pecans before serving.

Nutrition Information

- Calories: 102 calories
- Total Fat: 8.4 g
- Cholesterol: 15 mg
- Sodium: 42 mg
- Total Carbohydrate: 6.9 g

- Protein: 1 g

Classic Savory Deviled Eggs

"Hard-cooked eggs are stuffed with a creamy blend of mayonnaise, Dijon mustard and rice wine vinegar. Fresh dill and garlic powder add a delightful flavor."

Serving: 6 | Prep: 10 m | Ready in: 10 m

Ingredients

- 6 hard-cooked eggs, halved
- 1/4 cup mayonnaise
- 1 teaspoon rice wine vinegar
- 1/2 teaspoon chopped fresh dill
- 1 teaspoon Dijon mustard
- 1/4 teaspoon garlic powder
- 1/8 teaspoon salt
- 12 sprigs fresh dill (optional)

Direction

- Scoop egg yolks into a bowl and set egg whites aside. Mash yolks, mayonnaise, vinegar, 1/2 teaspoon chopped dill, Dijon mustard, garlic powder, and salt. Spoon yolk mixture into egg whites. Garnish with dill sprigs. Refrigerate until ready to serve.

Nutrition Information

- Calories: 139 calories
- Total Fat: 12.3 g
- Cholesterol: 189 mg
- Sodium: 192 mg
- Total Carbohydrate: 1 g

- Protein: 6.4 g

Corn Fritters

"Nothing warms up a cool night like a plateful of old-time corn fritters! Dig in, these are delicious!"

Serving: 12 | Prep: 10 m | Cook: 20 m | Ready in: 30 m

Ingredients

- 3 cups oil for frying
- 1 cup sifted all-purpose flour
- 1 teaspoon baking powder
- 1/2 teaspoon salt
- 1/4 teaspoon white sugar
- 1 egg, lightly beaten
- 1/2 cup milk
- 1 tablespoon shortening, melted
- 1 (12 ounce) can whole kernel corn, drained

Direction

- Heat oil in a heavy pot or deep fryer to 365 degrees F (185 degrees C).
- In a medium bowl, combine flour, baking powder, salt and sugar. Beat together egg, milk, and melted shortening; stir into flour mixture. Mix in the corn kernels.
- Drop fritter batter by spoonfuls into the hot oil, and fry until golden. Drain on paper towels.

Nutrition Information

- Calories: 133 calories
- Total Fat: 7.8 g
- Cholesterol: 18 mg

- Sodium: 224 mg
- Total Carbohydrate: 14 g
- Protein: 2.7 g

Country French Cheese

"This recipe can also be made with fat-free equivalents of cream cheese, shredded Cheddar and salad dressing to reduce the amount of calories. Serve with your favorite crackers."

Serving: 20

Ingredients

- 1/2 pound bacon - cooked and crumbled
- 1 pound cream cheese
- 1/2 pound shredded sharp Cheddar cheese
- 1/2 cup French dressing
- 1 cup chopped fresh parsley
- 1 cup chopped walnuts

Direction

- Place bacon in a large, deep skillet. Cook over medium high heat until evenly brown. Drain, crumble and set aside.
- In a large bowl, combine the bacon, cream cheese, Cheddar cheese and salad dressing. Mix together well and form into a ball.
- In a shallow dish, mix together the parsley and chopped walnuts. Roll cheese ball in mixture to coat. Refrigerate until chilled.

Nutrition Information

- Calories: 259 calories
- Total Fat: 23.3 g
- Cholesterol: 49 mg
- Sodium: 457 mg

- Total Carbohydrate: 2.9 g
- Protein: 9.7 g

Crab Stuffed Mushrooms

"This tasty appetizer seasoned with thyme, oregano, and savory. Choose good sized mushrooms, about 2 inches across. When cleaning mushrooms, don't run them under water. They are like little sponges, and will absorb it; just wipe them clean with a damp towel. The filling can be made with fresh, canned, or imitation crabmeat. If using canned, be sure to rinse it first."

Serving: 6 | Prep: 25 m | Cook: 15 m | Ready in: 40 m

Ingredients

- 1 pound fresh mushrooms
- 7 ounces crabmeat
- 5 green onions, thinly sliced
- 1/4 teaspoon dried thyme
- 1/4 teaspoon dried oregano
- 1/4 teaspoon ground savory
- ground black pepper to taste
- 1/4 cup grated Parmesan cheese
- 1/3 cup mayonnaise
- 3 tablespoons grated Parmesan cheese
- 1/4 teaspoon paprika

Direction

- Preheat the oven to 350 degrees F (175 degrees C).
- In a medium bowl, combine crabmeat, green onions, herbs, and pepper. Mix in mayonnaise and 1/4 cup Parmesan cheese until well combined. Refrigerate filling until ready for use.
- Wipe the mushrooms clean with a damp towel. Remove stems. Spoon out the gills and the base of the stem, making

deep cups. Discard gills and stems. Fill the mushroom caps with rounded teaspoonfuls of filling, and place them in an ungreased shallow baking dish. Sprinkle tops with Parmesan and paprika.
- Bake for 15 minutes. Remove from oven, and serve immediately

Nutrition Information

- Calories: 167 calories
- Total Fat: 12.1 g
- Cholesterol: 39 mg
- Sodium: 275 mg
- Total Carbohydrate: 4.2 g
- Protein: 11.7 g

Cranberry Brie Bites

"Tangy cranberry, creamy brie, and crunchy walnuts come together in a buttery shell for an appetizer that will wow your guests. Bonus: These can be made up to 3 days ahead; wrap them in plastic wrap before the baking step and store in the refrigerator. Serve warm or at room temperature."

Serving: 24 | Prep: 15 m | Cook: 18 m | Ready in: 1 h 23 m

Ingredients

- 1 (8 ounce) round Brie cheese, rind removed
- cooking spray
- 1 sheet frozen puff pastry, thawed
- 1/2 cup cranberry sauce
- 1/3 cup finely chopped walnuts
- sea salt to taste

Direction

- Place Brie cheese in the freezer for 20 minutes. Oil a mini muffin pan with cooking spray.
- Roll 1 puff pastry sheet out into a 10x14-inch rectangle. Cut the sheet lengthwise into 4 even strips and crosswise into 6 even strips; there should be 24 squares. Separate and press them gently into the muffin cups.
- Cut chilled Brie cheese into 24 pieces approximately 3/4-inch in size. Add 1 teaspoon cranberry sauce to each pastry-lined muffin cup; press in 1 piece of Brie and top with 1 teaspoon of chopped walnuts. Sprinkle bites with sea salt. Chill for at least 30 minutes and up to 3 days.
- Preheat oven to 400 degrees F (200 degrees C).

- Bake bites in the preheated oven until golden brown, 18 to 20 minutes.

Nutrition Information

- Calories: 106 calories
- Total Fat: 7.5 g
- Cholesterol: 9 mg
- Sodium: 99 mg
- Total Carbohydrate: 7 g
- Protein: 2.9 g

Cranberry Dip

"The color of this dip is very festive and would make a nice addition to any snack or appetizer table at your next holiday party."

Serving: 32 | Prep: 5 m | Cook: 20 m | Ready in: 8 h 25 m

Ingredients

- 1 (12 ounce) package fresh cranberries
- 1 cup white sugar
- 1 cup apricot jam
- 1 cup chopped pecans
- 1 (8 ounce) package cream cheese

Direction

- Preheat an oven to 350 degrees F (175 degrees C).
- Combine cranberries with sugar in a 2 quart baking dish with a lid, stirring well to coat all the berries. Bake in the preheated oven, covered, for about 30 minutes, until the cranberries pop and release their liquid.
- Remove from oven and stir in the apricot jam and pecans. Refrigerate overnight to blend the flavors. To serve, allow the cream cheese to come to room temperature, and pour dip over the block of cream cheese on a serving dish. Serve with buttery round crackers or small pretzels.

Nutrition Information

- Calories: 103 calories
- Total Fat: 5.2 g
- Cholesterol: 8 mg

- Sodium: 25 mg
- Total Carbohydrate: 14.7 g
- Protein: 1 g

Cranberry Jalapeno Cream Cheese Dip

"This is a fun dip that is both sweet and spicy. I got the recipe by varying other cranberry salsa and dip recipes I have found. I got the idea of the fusion of oil from a friend. There are many ideas for use and a great item to take along when you want to surprise your friends with something they probably have not tried. Serve with Triscuits®, pita chips, or crackers."

Serving: 16 | Prep: 10 m | Cook: 15 m | Ready in: 55 m

Ingredients

- 1/4 cup vegetable oil
- 10 ounces dried sweetened cranberries
- 1/2 cup white sugar, or to taste
- 1/2 cup water, or more as needed
- 2 small jalapeno peppers, seeded and finely diced
- 1 tablespoon lemon juice
- 2 teaspoons dried cilantro
- 1/4 teaspoon salt
- 2 (8 ounce) packages cream cheese, softened

Direction

- Heat a saucepan over medium heat; add oil. Stir cranberries into hot oil and cook until cranberries absorb most of oil, 5 to 10 minutes. Mix sugar, water, jalapeno peppers, lemon juice, cilantro, and salt into cranberries; cook until reduced and softened, 10 to 15 more minutes. Add more water if needed.
- Pulse cranberry mixture in a food processor or blender until very smooth; cool completely.

- Stir cooled cranberry mixture and cream cheese together in a bowl until smooth and creamy.

Nutrition Information

- Calories: 205 calories
- Total Fat: 13.2 g
- Cholesterol: 31 mg
- Sodium: 120 mg
- Total Carbohydrate: 21.7 g
- Protein: 2.2 g

Cranberry Meatballs

"This is a great recipe for people who would like to try something different for Thanksgiving. It makes a delicious side to any kind of turkey dish, and is very simple to make."

Serving: 7

Ingredients

- 2 pounds ground beef
- 1 cup bread crumbs
- 2 eggs, beaten
- 2 tablespoons soy sauce
- 1/4 teaspoon ground black pepper
- 1/2 teaspoon garlic powder
- 1/3 cup ketchup
- 1 (16 ounce) can jellied cranberry sauce
- 1 (18 ounce) bottle barbecue sauce
- 2 tablespoons brown sugar
- 1 tablespoon lemon juice

Direction

- Preheat oven to 350 degrees F. (175 degrees C).
- Mix together the hamburger, bread crumbs, eggs, soy sauce, pepper, garlic powder and ketchup. Form into small balls and bake for 30 minutes.
- In a saucepan over low heat, combine the cranberry sauce, barbecue sauce, brown sugar and lemon juice. Simmer and stir until smooth. Add meat balls and simmer for I hour. Serve warm.

Nutrition Information

- Calories: 718 calories
- Total Fat: 37 g
- Cholesterol: 163 mg
- Sodium: 1432 mg
- Total Carbohydrate: 69.6 g
- Protein: 26.1 g

Cranberry Relish Pizza

"This is a great take-along for a Thanksgiving or Christmas party."

Serving: 16 | Prep: 30 m | Cook: 10 m | Ready in: 1 h 40 m

Ingredients

- 2 (8 ounce) packages refrigerated crescent rolls
- 1 pinch white sugar, or more to taste
- 2 (12 ounce) packages fresh cranberries
- 2 large oranges - unpeeled, seeded, and chopped
- 1 1/2 cups chopped walnuts, or more to taste
- 2 (8 ounce) packages cream cheese, softened
- 1 cup plain Greek yogurt
- 1/4 cup honey
- 1/4 cup lemon juice
- 1 tablespoon vanilla extract

Direction

- Preheat oven to 375 degrees F (190 degrees C).
- Unroll crescent roll dough triangles and overlap slightly on a baking sheet, pinching the seams to join. Sprinkle lightly with sugar.
- Bake in the preheated oven until golden brown, 10 to 12 minutes. Set aside until completely cool.
- Chop cranberries, orange pieces, and walnuts in a food processor; sprinkle in sugar.
- Beat cream cheese, yogurt, honey, lemon juice, and vanilla extract in a large bowl with an electric mixer until fluffy.

- Spread cream cheese mixture evenly over the crust; smooth cranberry mixture on top. Cover with plastic wrap and chill until the cream cheese layer is firmer, about 30 minutes.

Nutrition Information

- Calories: 341 calories
- Total Fat: 23.4 g
- Cholesterol: 32 mg
- Sodium: 315 mg
- Total Carbohydrate: 27.1 g
- Protein: 7 g

Cranberry Salsa

"A fresh alternative to store-bought cranberry sauce. Quick and easy!"

Serving: 8 | Prep: 15 m | Ready in: 15 m

Ingredients

- 1 (12 ounce) bag fresh cranberries
- 6 tablespoons white sugar
- 2 tablespoons brandy-based orange liqueur (such as Grand Marnier®)
- 1/2 cucumber - peeled, seeded, and diced
- 2 stalks celery, chopped
- 4 slices pickled jalapeno pepper, finely chopped

Direction

- Place the cranberries into a food processor, and pulse until finely chopped. They should still have some texture. Transfer to a serving bowl, and stir in the sugar, orange liqueur, cucumber, celery and jalapeno. Let sit at room temperature for 15 minutes before serving to blend the flavors.

Nutrition Information

- Calories: 72 calories
- Total Fat: 0.1 g
- Cholesterol: 0 mg
- Sodium: 43 mg
- Total Carbohydrate: 16.9 g
- Protein: 0.3 g

Cream Cheese Ball

"Not a strong tasting cheese ball, children even like it."

Serving: 24 | Prep: 15 m | Ready in: 2 h 15 m

Ingredients

- 3 (8 ounce) packages cream cheese, softened
- 1 green bell pepper, chopped
- 3 green onions, minced
- 1 (8 ounce) can crushed pineapple with juice
- 1 tablespoon seasoning salt
- 2 cups finely chopped walnuts

Direction

- Place cream cheese in a medium size mixing bowl. Mix until cream cheese is soft. Mix in bell pepper, green onions, crushed pineapple, and seasoning salt.
- Line another mixing bowl with plastic wrap. Form the mixture into a ball and place it on the plastic wrap. Cover the bowl and refrigerate until the ball has set, 2 hours or more.
- When ready to serve, roll the cheese ball in the nuts and serve.

Nutrition Information

- Calories: 169 calories
- Total Fat: 16.2 g
- Cholesterol: 31 mg
- Sodium: 198 mg
- Total Carbohydrate: 4 g
- Protein: 3.7 g

Cream Cheese Penguins

"Just imagine a cute display of penguins, made with black olives, carrots and cream cheese! You can add scarves and hats by using fresh red pepper strips, or canned pimentos cut into different shapes. Use frilly toothpicks if you can."

Serving: 18 | Prep: 30 m | Ready in: 35 m

Ingredients

- 18 jumbo black olives, pitted
- 1 (8 ounce) package cream cheese, softened
- 18 small black olives
- 1 carrot

Direction

- Cut a slit from top to bottom, lengthwise, into the side of each jumbo olive. Carefully insert about 1 teaspoon of cream cheese into each olive. Slice the carrot into eighteen 1/4 inch thick rounds; cut a small notch out of each carrot slice to form feet. Save the cut out piece and press into center of small olive to form the beak. If necessary cut a small slit into each olive before inserting the beak.
- Set a big olive, large hole side down, onto a carrot slice. Then, set a small olive onto the large olive, adjusting so that the beak, cream cheese chest and notch in the carrot slice line up. Secure with a toothpick.

Nutrition Information

- Calories: 57 calories
- Total Fat: 5.5 g

- Cholesterol: 14 mg
- Sodium: 104 mg
- Total Carbohydrate: 1.2 g
- Protein: 1 g

Crispy Rosemary Sea Salt Flatbread Crackers

"Making your own 'fancy' crackers at home is a fairly basic operation, and not only will they be less expensive than store-bought, but you can customize them any way you want. Please pay attention to your baking time."

Serving: 8 | Prep: 20 m | Cook: 12 m | Ready in: 32 m

Ingredients

- 1 1/2 cups all-purpose flour
- 1 1/2 teaspoons kosher salt
- 1 teaspoon white sugar
- 1/2 cup freshly grated Parmigiano-Reggiano cheese
- 3 tablespoons extra-virgin olive oil
- 1/2 cup cold water
- 1 tablespoon minced fresh rosemary

Direction

- Preheat oven to 400 degrees F (200 degrees C). Line a baking sheet with a silicon mat or parchment paper.
- Place flour, salt, sugar, and grated cheese in a mixing bowl. Stir together until well mixed. Add rosemary; drizzle with olive oil and add water. Mix with a fork until mixture comes together in a fairly sticky dough and pulls away from the sides of the bowl, 3 to 5 minutes.
- Transfer dough onto floured surface and add flour as you knead the dough. Knead until it no longer sticks to work surface, 4 or minutes. Divide dough in half.
- Dust work surface with flour. Roll out dough to 1/8-inch thickness or less. Brush or mist surface of dough very lightly with water. Sprinkle with coarse sea salt. Prick the entire

- surface of dough with the tines of a fork to prevent crackers from puffing too much when baking.
- Cut each rolled out half into about 30 pieces with a pizza wheel. You can cut them out in squares, rectangles, or triangles--your choice. Transfer onto prepared baking sheet with a bench scraper or your floured fingers (dough will be very sticky).
- Bake in preheated oven until perfectly browned and crunchy, 10 to 15 minutes, depending on the thickness.

Nutrition Information

- Calories: 155 calories
- Total Fat: 6.7 g
- Cholesterol: 4 mg
- Sodium: 437 mg
- Total Carbohydrate: 18.7 g
- Protein: 4.4 g

DeepFried Stuffing

"If you thought leftover Thanksgiving stuffing was boring, this dish will change your mind! Any kind of stuffing (sausage, oyster, corn bread, or any variety of boxed) can be used. Heat up some gravy and bring on the cranberry sauce."

Serving: 6 | Prep: 20 m | Cook: 15 m | Ready in: 45 m

Ingredients

- 1/2 cup all-purpose flour
- 1 teaspoon poultry seasoning
- salt and ground black pepper to taste
- 2 eggs
- 2 tablespoons milk
- 1 cup seasoned bread crumbs
- 1/2 cup grated Parmesan cheese
- 1 teaspoon ground black pepper
- 2 1/2 cups prepared stuffing
- 1 quart oil for frying, or as needed

Direction

- Combine flour, poultry seasoning, salt, and black pepper to taste in a shallow bowl. Beat eggs and milk together in a second shallow bowl until smooth. Mix bread crumbs, Parmesan cheese, and 1 teaspoon black pepper together in a third shallow bowl.
- Scoop stuffing, about 2 tablespoons per serving, and roll into a ball using your hands, forming about 12 balls. Dredge each ball through the flour mixture, shaking off any excess. Transfer each ball to the egg mixture and evenly coat. Roll each ball in the bread crumbs mixture until evenly coated.

- Set each stuffing ball on a plate and allow to sit for the coating to stick to the stuffing.
- Heat oil in a deep-fryer or large saucepan to 350 degrees F (175 degrees C).
- Carefully lower 4 to 5 stuffing balls into the hot oil and fry until golden brown on all sides, about 4 minutes; transfer to a paper towel-lined plate using a slotted spoon. Repeat with the remaining stuffing balls.

Nutrition Information

- Calories: 448 calories
- Total Fat: 26.7 g
- Cholesterol: 68 mg
- Sodium: 958 mg
- Total Carbohydrate: 40.7 g
- Protein: 11.5 g

Deviled Eggs

"These deviled eggs are made with Miracle Whip® instead of mayo."

Serving: 8

Ingredients

- 8 eggs
- 1/2 teaspoon prepared mustard
- 1 tablespoon creamy salad dressing (such as Miracle Whip®), or as needed
- salt and pepper to taste
- 1 pinch paprika

Direction

- Place eggs in saucepan and cover with water. Bring to boil. Cover, remove from heat, and let eggs sit in hot water for 10 to 12 minutes. Remove from hot water and cool in ice water.
- Peel and cut in half lengthwise. Remove yolks and combine with mustard, salad dressing and salt and pepper. Mix together until smooth.
- Refill each egg half with the yolk mixture and sprinkle with paprika.

Nutrition Information

- Calories: 77 calories
- Total Fat: 5.5 g
- Cholesterol: 187 mg
- Sodium: 88 mg
- Total Carbohydrate: 0.7 g

- Protein: 6.3 g

Deviled Eggs I

"Another recipe passed down to me by my mother. Very good!"

Serving: 6 | Prep: 20 m | Ready in: 20 m

Ingredients

- 6 eggs
- 1/2 teaspoon paprika
- 2 tablespoons mayonnaise
- 1/2 teaspoon mustard powder

Direction

- Place eggs in a pot of salted water. Bring the water to a boil, and let eggs cook in boiling water until they are hard boiled, approximately 10 to 15 minutes. Drain eggs, and let cool.
- Cut eggs in half, lengthwise. Remove the egg yolks and mash them together in a small mixing bowl. Mix in the paprika, mayonnaise, and dry mustard. Spoon mixture into the egg whites; cool and serve.

Nutrition Information

- Calories: 107 calories
- Total Fat: 8.7 g
- Cholesterol: 188 mg
- Sodium: 96 mg
- Total Carbohydrate: 0.7 g
- Protein: 6.4 g

Dried Fruit Cheese Ball

"A different twist for a wonderful cheese ball. I got this recipe from a co-worker's wife. Thanks Maggie!"

Serving: 6 | Prep: 10 m | Ready in: 3 h 10 m

Ingredients

- 1 (8 ounce) package cream cheese, softened
- 2 tablespoons honey
- 1/2 (8 ounce) package mild Cheddar cheese, shredded
- 1 (6 ounce) package dried mixed fruit, chopped
- 1 cup chopped pecans

Direction

- In a medium bowl combine cream cheese and honey; beat until smooth. Stir in cheese and chopped fruit; mix well.
- Form into a ball and roll in chopped nuts. Chill for at least 3 hours.

Nutrition Information

- Calories: 424 calories
- Total Fat: 32.4 g
- Cholesterol: 61 mg
- Sodium: 232 mg
- Total Carbohydrate: 28.5 g
- Protein: 9.9 g

Easy Awesome Shrimp Scampi

"This is a recipe that my Mom makes on holidays but is great any time of the year. This is an awesome recipe and very easy to make"

Serving: 8 | Prep: 10 m | Cook: 45 m | Ready in: 55 m

Ingredients

- 1 cup butter
- 1 pound cooked small salad shrimp
- 2 sleeves buttery round crackers (such as Ritz®), crushed
- 3 tablespoons lemon juice
- 4 teaspoons garlic powder

Direction

- Preheat oven to 250 degrees F (120 degrees C).
- Melt butter in a saucepan over medium heat. Fold shrimp into melted butter to coat. Mix cracker crumbs, lemon juice, and garlic powder into shrimp; transfer into a 9-inch square baking dish. Cover dish with aluminum foil.
- Bake in the preheated oven until bubbling, about 45 minutes.

Nutrition Information

- Calories: 410 calories
- Total Fat: 31.5 g
- Cholesterol: 172 mg
- Sodium: 547 mg
- Total Carbohydrate: 18 g
- Protein: 14 g

Easy Baked Brie with Almonds and Brown Sugar

"This baked Brie is my go-to recipe when I have to make something elegant, tasteful, and extremely easy when entertaining guests."

Serving: 6 | Prep: 10 m | Cook: 8 m | Ready in: 23 m

Ingredients

- 1/2 cup sliced almonds, divided
- 1/2 cup packed brown sugar
- 1 tablespoon Dijon mustard
- 1 (8 ounce) round Brie cheese
- 1 French baguette
- cooking spray

Direction

- Preheat oven to 425 degrees F (220 degrees C).
- Coarsely chop 1/4 cup almonds. Combine chopped almonds, brown sugar, and mustard in a bowl; mix well.
- Cut Brie round horizontally in half. Place 1 half cut-side up in the center of a round baking stone. Spread half of the sugar mixture evenly over Brie. Top with the remaining half, cut-side up, and spread remaining sugar mixture on top. Sprinkle with remaining 1/4 cup sliced almonds.
- Cut baguette diagonally in slices. Arrange slices around Brie and spray with cooking spray.
- Bake in the preheated oven until baguette slices are golden brown and Brie begins to soften, 8 to 10 minutes. Remove from oven and let stand 5 minutes before serving.

Nutrition Information

- Calories: 363 calories
- Total Fat: 11.5 g
- Cholesterol: 38 mg
- Sodium: 674 mg
- Total Carbohydrate: 50.7 g
- Protein: 14.5 g

Easy Pumpkin Dip

"This is a great recipe for fall. Serve with sliced apples."

Serving: 12 | Prep: 10 m | Ready in: 40 m

Ingredients

- 3/4 cup low-fat cream cheese
- 1/2 cup packed brown sugar
- 1/2 cup canned pumpkin
- 2 teaspoons maple syrup
- 1/2 teaspoon ground cinnamon

Direction

- Beat cream cheese, brown sugar, and canned pumpkin together with an electric mixer on medium speed in a bowl until light and creamy, 3 to 5 minutes. Add maple syrup and cinnamon and beat until smooth, 1 to 2 minutes. Cover with plastic wrap and refrigerate for 30 minutes.

Nutrition Information

- Calories: 78 calories
- Total Fat: 2.9 g
- Cholesterol: 9 mg
- Sodium: 50 mg
- Total Carbohydrate: 11.7 g
- Protein: 1.9 g

Festive Cheese Dip Slaw

"Festive appetizer served in hollowed out whole red cabbage -- accompanied by corn chips! Beautiful, easy, and oh so tasty! Especially pretty for Thanksgiving and Christmas appetizer buffets. Best if made ahead at least 24 hours to let flavors blend (can refrigerate in covered container for up to one week). Even with peppers, this dip is not too spicy -- children love this dip. A winner!"

Serving: 36 | Prep: 30 m | Ready in: 1 d 30 m

Ingredients

- 1 pound coarsely shredded Swiss cheese
- 1 bunch green onions, chopped
- 1/2 cup chopped banana peppers
- 1/2 cup seeded and finely chopped jalapeno peppers (wear gloves)
- 1/2 cup mayonnaise, or as needed
- 1 head red cabbage

Direction

- In a bowl, lightly mix the Swiss cheese, green onions, banana peppers, jalapeno peppers, and mayonnaise. Cover and refrigerate 24 hours to blend flavors. Mix in more mayonnaise before serving, if desired.
- To serve, cut core out of cabbage and discard. Cut a thick slice from the bottom of the cabbage; use a fork to pull the inner leaves out of the cabbage to leave a hollowed out bowl. Pull several of the outer leaves slightly open and fold them back to make the bowl more attractive; serve the chilled dip in the hollowed cabbage.

Nutrition Information

- Calories: 79 calories
- Total Fat: 6 g
- Cholesterol: 13 mg
- Sodium: 49 mg
- Total Carbohydrate: 3.1 g
- Protein: 3.9 g

Festive Cracker Spread

"All I have to say is this recipe is addictive. You will feel a stronger than normal gravitational pull toward this dip. Serve with crackers. Beware and Enjoy!"

Serving: 20 | Prep: 20 m | Ready in: 1 h 20 m

Ingredients

- 1 (8 ounce) package cream cheese, softened
- 1 (8 ounce) package finely shredded sharp Cheddar cheese
- 1/2 cup mayonnaise
- 3/4 cup chopped pimento-stuffed olives
- 1/2 cup chopped celery
- 1/3 cup chopped onion
- 1/4 cup chopped green bell pepper
- 2 teaspoons dried parsley

Direction

- Beat the cream cheese, Cheddar cheese, and mayonnaise with an electric mixer in a bowl until smooth. Fold in the olives, celery, onion, bell pepper, and parsley; mixing just enough to evenly combine. Cover and chill for at least 1 hour.

Nutrition Information

- Calories: 134 calories
- Total Fat: 12.9 g
- Cholesterol: 26 mg
- Sodium: 310 mg
- Total Carbohydrate: 1.2 g

- Protein: 3.9 g

Feta Cheese Foldovers

"Golden puffed pastries are filled with a feta cheese mixture. These can be made ahead, and popped into the oven after your guests arrive."

Serving: 12 | Prep: 20 m | Cook: 20 m | Ready in: 40 m

Ingredients

- 8 ounces feta cheese, crumbled
- 3 tablespoons finely chopped green onions
- 1 egg, beaten
- 1 (17.5 ounce) package frozen puff pastry, thawed
- 1 egg yolk, beaten with 1 teaspoon water

Direction

- Preheat oven to 375 degrees F (190 degrees C).
- In a small bowl, blend feta cheese, green onions, and egg. Cut pastry into 12 (3 inch) squares. Place a mounded tablespoon of feta mixture in the center of each square. Moisten edges with water, and fold pastry over filling to form a triangle. Press edges together firmly with a fork to seal. Lightly brush pastries with the egg yolk mixture.
- Bake for 20 minutes in the preheated oven, or until golden brown. Serve warm or at room temperature.

Nutrition Information

- Calories: 286 calories
- Total Fat: 20.4 g
- Cholesterol: 49 mg

- Sodium: 319 mg
- Total Carbohydrate: 19.4 g
- Protein: 6.4 g

Fluffy Fruit Dip

"This is a delicious fluffy orange flavored dip for skewered fruit. It is equally good spooned over cubes of fruit and served as a first course or dessert. Orange juice may be substituted for the liqueur."

Serving: 16

Ingredients

- 1 (7 ounce) jar marshmallow creme
- 1 (8 ounce) package cream cheese, softened
- 1 orange, zested
- 1 fluid ounce orange liqueur

Direction

- In a large bowl, fold together the marshmallow creme and cream cheese.
- Stir in grated zest and liqueur or juice. Refrigerate until chilled.

Nutrition Information

- Calories: 95 calories
- Total Fat: 4.9 g
- Cholesterol: 15 mg
- Sodium: 51 mg
- Total Carbohydrate: 10.9 g
- Protein: 1.2 g

Fruit Dip

"Great with fresh fruit! Use apples, pineapple chunks, grapes, oranges or other fruits of your choice. Have toothpicks available to spear the fruit for dipping. Great for showers or parties!"

Serving: 24

Ingredients

- 8 ounces cream cheese
- 1/2 cup marshmallow creme
- 2 cups frozen whipped topping, thawed
- 1/4 cup unsweetened pineapple juice

Direction

- Blend together the cream cheese, marshmallow cream and thawed topping. Add enough pineapple juice to make it dipping consistency. Chill for 1 hour.

Nutrition Information

- Calories: 57 calories
- Total Fat: 4.2 g
- Cholesterol: 10 mg
- Sodium: 30 mg
- Total Carbohydrate: 3.5 g
- Protein: 0.7 g

Glazed Nuts

"Glazed nuts are a favorite holiday snack, and are very simple to make. Use walnuts, pecans, almonds, or a mix."

Serving: 16 | Prep: 15 m | Cook: 30 m | Ready in: 45 m

Ingredients

- 1 egg white
- 1/2 cup packed brown sugar
- 2 tablespoons ground cinnamon
- 1 teaspoon ground cloves
- 1 teaspoon ground ginger
- 1 tablespoon vanilla extract
- 1 pound walnut halves

Direction

- Preheat oven to 300 degrees F (150 degrees C). Coat a baking sheet with cooking spray.
- In a large bowl, beat egg white until foamy. Stir in brown sugar, cinnamon, cloves, ginger, and vanilla. Add nuts, and stir to coat. Spread evenly onto prepared pan.
- Bake for 30 minutes, stirring occasionally, or until well toasted and golden brown. Remove from oven, and cool completely. Store in an airtight container.

Nutrition Information

- Calories: 218 calories
- Total Fat: 18.5 g
- Cholesterol: 0 mg
- Sodium: 6 mg

- Total Carbohydrate: 11.6 g
- Protein: 4.6 g

Grammies Cranberry Salsa

"Grammie makes this for Thanksgiving every year and it is such a big hit. It goes great with snack breads, crackers, biscuits, rolls and veggies. Hope you enjoy it as much as we do. "

Serving: 10 | Prep: 15 m | Ready in: 15 m

Ingredients

- 1 (6 ounce) can frozen orange juice concentrate, thawed and undiluted
- 1 cup cranberries, coarsely chopped
- 2 yellow bell peppers, chopped
- 1 fresh red chile pepper, chopped
- 1 red onion, chopped
- 1 clove garlic, finely chopped
- 1/2 cup fresh cilantro leaves
- 1/4 teaspoon ground cumin, or to taste

Direction

- Mix frozen orange juice concentrate, cranberries, yellow bell peppers, red chile pepper, red onion, garlic, cilantro, and cumin seeds together in a serving dish. Stir to combine.

Nutrition Information

- Calories: 52 calories
- Total Fat: 0.2 g
- Cholesterol: 0 mg
- Sodium: 3 mg
- Total Carbohydrate: 12.4 g
- Protein: 1.1 g

Grandmas Stuffed Celery

"My grandma always made stuffed celery at Thanksgiving and Christmas. As kids, we were always so hungry before the holiday meal we would sneak and get a piece of celery to curb our appetite. It was nearly all gone by meal time and we always got fussed at with hint of a grin from Grandma. Now I never have holiday meals without it!"

Serving: 24 | Prep: 30 m | Ready in: 30 m

Ingredients

- 1 bunch celery - large stalks washed, trimmed, and cut into 3 sections
- 2 (8 ounce) packages cream cheese at room temperature
- 3/4 cup chopped pimento-stuffed green olives
- 2 cloves garlic, finely minced
- 1 pinch salt and freshly cracked black pepper to taste

Direction

- Thoroughly dry each piece of celery with paper towels. Mix the cream cheese, olives, garlic, salt, and black pepper in a bowl. Using a knife, spread a generous amount of cream cheese filling down the center indentation of each celery piece. Serve immediately or refrigerate.

Nutrition Information

- Calories: 76 calories
- Total Fat: 7.3 g
- Cholesterol: 21 mg
- Sodium: 225 mg

- Total Carbohydrate: 1.4 g
- Protein: 1.7 g

Grilled Oysters with Fennel Butter

"A seasonal side dish or appetizer with fresh oysters and fennel."

Serving: 24

Ingredients

- 1 teaspoon fennel seed, ground
- 1 cup butter, softened
- 1 tablespoon shallots, minced
- 1 tablespoon chopped fennel greens
- 1 teaspoon ground black pepper
- 1/2 teaspoon salt
- 24 unopened, fresh, live medium oysters

Direction

- Prepare and light a grill or preheat the oven to 500 degrees F (260 degrees C).
- In a small bowl, blend together the butter, ground fennel seeds, shallots, fennel bulb, fennel greens, pepper and salt.
- Arrange the oysters on the grill or oven rack, cover and cook for 3 to 5 minutes or until they start hissing and begin to open.
- Using an oyster knife, pry each oyster open at the hinge, loosen the oyster and discard the flat shell. Top each oyster with 1/2 teaspoon of the fennel butter. Return to grill and cook until butter is melted and hot.

Nutrition Information

- Calories: 77 calories
- Total Fat: 7.8 g

- Cholesterol: 24 mg
- Sodium: 110 mg
- Total Carbohydrate: 0.5 g
- Protein: 1.6 g

Heavenly Shrimp Dip

"This shrimp and cream cheese dip is easy to prepare and always popular. For best results, serve the cream cheese at room temperature and the cocktail sauce well chilled."

Serving: 4

Ingredients

- 2 (8 ounce) packages cream cheese
- 1 (8 ounce) jar cocktail sauce
- 1/2 pound shrimp, peeled and deveined
- 1 lime
- 1 (16 ounce) package buttery round crackers

Direction

- Place cream cheese in center of serving platter.
- Mix together cocktail sauce and shrimp. Pour mixture over cream cheese.
- Slice lime in half; squeeze one half over cocktail sauce. Slice other half into wedges for garnish.
- Place crackers and lime wedges around edge of plate and serve.

Nutrition Information

- Calories: 1086 calories
- Total Fat: 71.9 g
- Cholesterol: 209 mg
- Sodium: 2121 mg
- Total Carbohydrate: 82.4 g
- Protein: 27.7 g

Herman Reunion Cheese Ball

"The requests for this family recipe never stop, so here it is for everybody to enjoy. These cheese balls freeze well for months and make wonderful holiday gifts. To give the balls as gifts: wrap each ball or log individually in festive holiday plastic wrap."

Serving: 12 | Prep: 15 m | Ready in: 15 m

Ingredients

- 3 (8 ounce) packages cream cheese, softened
- 1/2 teaspoon minced garlic
- 1 tablespoon Worcestershire sauce
- 1 tablespoon hot pepper sauce
- 1 pound shredded Cheddar cheese
- 1 cup pecans, coarsely chopped
- 1/4 cup chopped fresh parsley

Direction

- In an electric food processor or blender, combine cream cheese, garlic, Worcestershire sauce and hot pepper sauce. Blend well. Add Cheddar cheese and process until the Cheddar is fine, but still very visible. Shape the mixture into balls or logs. Wrap individually in plastic wrap and place in the freezer.
- While the balls are in the freezer, combine the ground pecans and parsley in a shallow bowl. Remove the balls from the freezer and roll them in the pecan and parsley mixture.

Nutrition Information

- Calories: 413 calories

- Total Fat: 38.6 g
- Cholesterol: 101 mg
- Sodium: 416 mg
- Total Carbohydrate: 3.7 g
- Protein: 14.5 g

Holiday Crabmeat Ball

"Tasty and quick imitation crabmeat appetizer sure to please a crowd. Prepare with enough time to chill! This tastes best with the addition of Tiger Sauce. If you cannot find it (usually in the ketchup/condiment section) and use cocktail sauce instead, remember cocktail sauce contains horseradish and adjust your ingredients accordingly!"

Serving: 25 | Prep: 10 m | Ready in: 1 h 10 m

Ingredients

- 2 pounds imitation crabmeat, flaked
- 2 (8 ounce) packages reduced-fat cream cheese
- 1 onion, diced
- 2 tablespoons prepared horseradish, or to taste
- 2 tablespoons Worcestershire sauce
- 1 (12 ounce) jar cocktail sauce

Direction

- Pulse crabmeat in a food processor several times until minced. Transfer crabmeat to a large bowl. Blend cream cheese in food processor until creamy. Add onion, horseradish, and Worcestershire sauce to cream cheese; blend until smooth.
- Stir cream cheese mixture into crab mixture until well-combined. For crab mixture into 2 to 3 balls, cover with plastic wrap, and refrigerate until firm and chilled, at least 1 hour. Place crab balls on a platter and top with cocktail sauce.

Nutrition Information

- Calories: 94 calories
- Total Fat: 3.5 g
- Cholesterol: 17 mg
- Sodium: 540 mg
- Total Carbohydrate: 10.6 g
- Protein: 5 g

Hot Artichoke and Spinach Dip II

"This dip is amazing -- so cheesy and fragrant. If you don't like artichokes, don't worry -- you'll never know they're in there! My only question is: Is it okay to just eat it with a spoon right out of the dish?"

Serving: 12 | Prep: 15 m | Cook: 25 m | Ready in: 40 m

Ingredients

- 1 (8 ounce) package cream cheese, softened
- 1/4 cup mayonnaise
- 1/4 cup grated Parmesan cheese
- 1/4 cup grated Romano cheese
- 1 clove garlic, peeled and minced
- 1/2 teaspoon dried basil
- 1/4 teaspoon garlic salt
- salt and pepper to taste
- 1 (14 ounce) can artichoke hearts, drained and chopped
- 1/2 cup frozen chopped spinach, thawed and drained
- 1/4 cup shredded mozzarella cheese

Direction

- Preheat oven to 350 degrees F (175 degrees C). Lightly grease a small baking dish.
- In a medium bowl, mix together cream cheese, mayonnaise, Parmesan cheese, Romano cheese, garlic, basil, garlic salt, salt and pepper. Gently stir in artichoke hearts and spinach.
- Transfer the mixture to the prepared baking dish. Top with mozzarella cheese. Bake in the preheated oven 25 minutes, until bubbly and lightly browned.

Nutrition Information

- Calories: 134 calories
- Total Fat: 11.7 g
- Cholesterol: 28 mg
- Sodium: 315 mg
- Total Carbohydrate: 3.4 g
- Protein: 4.4 g

Hot Artichoke Dip

"This is a wonderful appetizer or dip that is not truly hot, but it is easy, cheesy and great! Serve with crackers, toast or vegetables."

Serving: 32 | Prep: 10 m | Cook: 25 m | Ready in: 35 m

Ingredients

- 2/3 cup Parmesan cheese
- 2/3 cup mayonnaise
- 1/3 cup heavy whipping cream
- 1 (14 ounce) can artichoke hearts, drained and chopped
- 2 tablespoons thinly sliced green onion
- 1 tablespoon chopped pimento peppers

Direction

- Preheat oven to 325 degrees F (165 degrees C). Lightly grease a medium baking dish.
- Blend together the cheese, mayonnaise and whipping cream. Stir in the artichokes, green onions and pimentos. Mix well, and transfer to the prepared baking dish.
- Bake 25 minutes in the preheated oven, until lightly browned.

Nutrition Information

- Calories: 57 calories
- Total Fat: 5.2 g
- Cholesterol: 7 mg
- Sodium: 133 mg
- Total Carbohydrate: 1.7 g

- Protein: 1.3 g

Hot Crab Dip

"This delicious, addictive crab dip will have your family begging for more. Serve as an appetizer with onion or garlic crackers."

Serving: 40 | Prep: 10 m | Cook: 30 m | Ready in: 40 m

Ingredients

- 2 (8 ounce) packages cream cheese, softened
- 4 tablespoons mayonnaise
- 2 cups shredded Cheddar cheese
- 2 (6 ounce) cans crabmeat
- 1 1/2 tablespoons fresh lemon juice
- 2 teaspoons hot sauce
- 2 tablespoons Worcestershire sauce
- paprika, for garnish

Direction

- Preheat oven to 350 degrees F (175 degrees C).
- In a medium bowl, mix the cream cheese, mayonnaise, Cheddar cheese, crabmeat, lemon juice, hot sauce and Worcestershire sauce. Transfer to a shallow 9x13 inch baking dish. Garnish with paprika.
- Bake in the preheated oven 30 minutes, or until golden brown and bubbly.

Nutrition Information

- Calories: 81 calories
- Total Fat: 7 g
- Cholesterol: 26 mg
- Sodium: 119 mg

- Total Carbohydrate: 0.6 g
- Protein: 4 g

Hot Spinach Red Pepper Dip

"A cheesy and creamy hot dip best served in a bread bowl or spread on toasted bread."

Serving: 8 | Prep: 5 m | Cook: 20 m | Ready in: 25 m

Ingredients

- 1 cup water
- 1 cup diced red bell pepper
- 1/2 cup thawed frozen chopped spinach
- 1 (8 ounce) package cream cheese
- 2 tablespoons milk
- 1/2 cup grated Parmesan cheese
- 1/2 teaspoon crushed red pepper flakes
- 1/4 teaspoon salt
- 1 pinch freshly ground black pepper
- 1 tablespoon finely diced red bell pepper

Direction

- Bring the cup of water to a boil in a small saucepan over high heat and add the 1 cup of diced red pepper and the chopped spinach. Bring the water back to a boil, turn the heat down to medium and simmer until the pepper is very soft, about 10 minutes. Drain the spinach and red pepper in a colander, pressing out as much liquid as possible.
- Combine the cream cheese and milk in the saucepan and cook over medium heat until hot and softened. Stir in the cooked spinach and red peppers, Parmesan cheese, crushed

red pepper flakes, salt, and ground black pepper. Continue to stir until well combined and heated through.
- Spoon hot dip into a serving dish and serve with the tablespoon of finely diced red bell pepper sprinkled on top for garnish.

Nutrition Information

- Calories: 131 calories
- Total Fat: 11.4 g
- Cholesterol: 36 mg
- Sodium: 243 mg
- Total Carbohydrate: 2.9 g
- Protein: 4.7 g

Jalapeno Popper Cups

"Didn't have enough Jalapenos to make full out poppers, but improvised for a creamy and spicy appetizer. You'll want to eat them right away, but they will be molten hot so be careful!"

Serving: 12 | Prep: 10 m | Cook: 20 m | Ready in: 30 m

Ingredients

- 12 mini phyllo tart shells
- 4 ounces cream cheese, softened
- 1/2 cup shredded Cheddar cheese
- 2 jalapeno peppers, seeded and chopped
- 1 tablespoon hot pepper sauce
- bacon bits

Direction

- Preheat an oven to 350 degrees F (175 degrees C). Place phyllo cups onto a baking sheet.
- Stir together cream cheese, Cheddar cheese, jalapenos, and hot sauce in a bowl. Spoon mixture into phyllo cups. Sprinkle bacon bits on top. Bake in preheated oven until golden brown, about 15 to 20 minutes. Serve warm.

Nutrition Information

- Calories: 81 calories
- Total Fat: 6.2 g
- Cholesterol: 17 mg
- Sodium: 153 mg
- Total Carbohydrate: 3 g
- Protein: 3.2 g

Jamies Baked Brie

"My ex-wife Jamie's been making this savory Brie en croute since way back before we were married. I think she must have gotten the idea from a magazine, but I've never seen the recipe... I just wing it. It can be made with either puff pastry sheets (quick and easy) or phyllo sheets (more work, flakier shell). Serve with fancy table crackers or digestive biscuits."

Serving: 25 | Prep: 15 m | Cook: 20 m | Ready in: 35 m

Ingredients

- 1 shallot, minced
- 2 cloves garlic, minced
- 1/4 teaspoon white pepper
- 1 tablespoon dry vermouth
- 1 (8 ounce) round Brie cheese
- 3 sheets phyllo dough
- 2 tablespoons melted butter

Direction

- Preheat an oven to 350 degrees F (175 degrees C).
- Stir the shallot, garlic, white pepper, and vermouth together in a small bowl; set aside. Cut the rind off the top of the brie cheese, leaving a 1/4-inch lip around the edge. Place the brie cheese onto a baking sheet, and spoon the shallot mixture over top. Fold the phyllo sheets in half to make square pieces. Wrap the brie with the phyllo squares, tucking the edges underneath of the brie cheese. Trim the corners if needed to avoid tucking too much pastry underneath. You want complete enclosure, but without too much overlap.

Brush the top with melted butter to make the pastry brown in the oven.
- Bake in the preheated oven until the phyllo has turned golden brown and the brie cheese is very soft, about 20 minutes. Serve warm.

Nutrition Information

- Calories: 48 calories
- Total Fat: 3.6 g
- Cholesterol: 12 mg
- Sodium: 75 mg
- Total Carbohydrate: 1.8 g
- Protein: 2.1 g

Kosher Pineapple Cranberry Salsa Pareve

"Fresh fruit, jalapeno, and onion combine to produce a sweet and spicy salsa perfect for turkey, chicken, or pork."

Serving: 12 | Prep: 20 m | Cook: 5 m | Ready in: 1 h 25 m

Ingredients

- 1 (12 ounce) bag fresh cranberries
- 1 cup white sugar
- 1/2 cup water
- 1 fresh pineapple - peeled, cored, and cut into small chunks
- 1 mango - peeled, seeded, and diced
- 1 bunch cilantro, chopped
- 3 Satsuma mandarin oranges, peeled and segmented
- 1 sweet onion, diced
- 1 jalapeno pepper, diced
- 1/4 cup orange juice

Direction

- Cook and gently stir cranberries, sugar, and water in a large skillet over medium heat until the mixture begins to bubble. Reduce heat to low and cook until cranberries begin to soften and break down, about 5 minutes. Remove from heat and cool to room temperature.
- Combine pineapple, mango, cilantro, mandarin oranges, onion, and jalapeno together in a bowl; drizzle with orange juice. Stir cooled cranberries and pineapple mixture together. Refrigerate until chilled, at least 1 hour.

Nutrition Information

- Calories: 164 calories
- Total Fat: 0.3 g
- Cholesterol: 0 mg
- Sodium: 5 mg
- Total Carbohydrate: 42.4 g
- Protein: 1.2 g

Kristas Queso

"I always make this at Christmas, Thanksgiving, birthdays, and football parties. It is great, easy, and goes fast."

Serving: 24 | Prep: 10 m | Cook: 40 m | Ready in: 50 m

Ingredients

- 1 (16 ounce) package bulk pork breakfast sausage
- 1 (16 ounce) package processed cheese food, cubed
- 1 (4 ounce) jar mushrooms, drained
- 1 (14 ounce) can diced tomatoes with green chile peppers, drained

Direction

- Cook the sausage in a large skillet over medium heat until completely browned; drain.
- Combine the cooked sausage, cheese, mushrooms, and diced tomatoes with green chile peppers in a slow cooker. Set slow cooker to Low. Cook until the cheese melts completely, stirring occasionally, 30 to 40 minutes.

Nutrition Information

- Calories: 153 calories
- Total Fat: 13.5 g
- Cholesterol: 30 mg
- Sodium: 491 mg
- Total Carbohydrate: 1.3 g
- Protein: 6.6 g

Microwave Spiced Nuts

"This is a great candied nut recipe I stole from my mom. She likes walnuts, I like pecans. It's dead easy and my wife says she needs to leave the house when I make them, so she won't eat them all! Try experimenting with the spices, maybe clove or allspice!"

Serving: 12 | Prep: 5 m | Cook: 7 m | Ready in: 12 m

Ingredients

- 1/4 cup butter
- 1/2 cup brown sugar
- 1/2 teaspoon ground nutmeg
- 1 teaspoon ground cinnamon
- 2 tablespoons water
- 3 cups pecan halves

Direction

- Melt butter in a 4 quart glass casserole dish in the microwave. Stir in the brown sugar, nutmeg, cinnamon and water. Microwave on high for 1 minute. Stir in the nuts so they are well coated. Microwave for 4 to 5 additional minutes on high, stirring every minute. Spread cooked nuts out onto parchment or waxed paper to cool.

Nutrition Information

- Calories: 245 calories
- Total Fat: 23.3 g
- Cholesterol: 10 mg
- Sodium: 29 mg
- Total Carbohydrate: 9.9 g
- Protein: 2.5 g

Momma Hallmarks Cheese Balls

"Grandmother Hallmark's cheese ball recipe has been a family holiday favorite for decades."

Serving: 45 | Prep: 15 m | Cook: 15 m | Ready in: 50 m

Ingredients

- 1 pound shredded extra-sharp Cheddar cheese
- 1 pound margarine, softened
- 5 cups all-purpose flour
- 1 cup toasted chopped pecans
- 1 teaspoon salt
- 1 (16 ounce) package confectioners' sugar

Direction

- Preheat oven to 375 degrees F (190 degrees C).
- Mix Cheddar cheese and margarine together in a large bowl until well-combined. Add flour, pecans, and salt; stir until dough is well-mixed. Roll into 1- to 2-inch balls and place on a baking sheet.
- Bake in the preheated oven until golden brown, 15 to 20 minutes. Cool completely.
- Pour confectioners' sugar into a shallow bowl; roll cooled cheese balls in sugar to coat completely.

Nutrition Information

- Calories: 219 calories
- Total Fat: 13.4 g
- Cholesterol: 11 mg
- Sodium: 211 mg
- Total Carbohydrate: 21.3 g
- Protein: 4.3 g

Mouth Watering Stuffed Mushrooms

"These delicious mushrooms taste just like restaurant-style stuffed mushrooms and are my guy's absolute favorite."

Serving: 12 | Prep: 25 m | Cook: 20 m | Ready in: 45 m

Ingredients

- 12 whole fresh mushrooms
- 1 tablespoon vegetable oil
- 1 tablespoon minced garlic
- 1 (8 ounce) package cream cheese, softened
- 1/4 cup grated Parmesan cheese
- 1/4 teaspoon ground black pepper
- 1/4 teaspoon onion powder
- 1/4 teaspoon ground cayenne pepper

Direction

- Preheat oven to 350 degrees F (175 degrees C). Spray a baking sheet with cooking spray. Clean mushrooms with a damp paper towel. Carefully break off stems. Chop stems extremely fine, discarding tough end of stems.
- Heat oil in a large skillet over medium heat. Add garlic and chopped mushroom stems to the skillet. Fry until any moisture has disappeared, taking care not to burn garlic. Set aside to cool.
- When garlic and mushroom mixture is no longer hot, stir in cream cheese, Parmesan cheese, black pepper, onion powder and cayenne pepper. Mixture should be very thick. Using a little spoon, fill each mushroom cap with a generous amount of stuffing. Arrange the mushroom caps on prepared cookie sheet.

- Bake for 20 minutes in the preheated oven, or until the mushrooms are piping hot and liquid starts to form under caps.

Nutrition Information

- Calories: 88 calories
- Total Fat: 8.2 g
- Cholesterol: 22 mg
- Sodium: 82 mg
- Total Carbohydrate: 1.5 g
- Protein: 2.7 g

Olive Puffs

"These puff pastry-wrapped olives are our family's favorite holiday appetizer. We make them with a variety of olives - pimento stuffed green, plump kalamata, Provencal - just make sure they are pitted. We like to use strongly flavored olives; the flavor of canned ripe olives disappears in the puff pastry. You can make these ahead, and freeze; allow 30 minutes for the pastry to thaw before baking. Another advantage: the kids like to make them and eat them."

Serving: 12 | Prep: 20 m | Cook: 20 m | Ready in: 40 m

Ingredients

- 24 pimento-stuffed green olives
- 1 (17.25 ounce) package frozen puff pastry, thawed

Direction

- Preheat oven to 400 degrees F (200 degrees C).
- Cut pastry into strips about 6 inches long and 1/2 inch wide. Wrap a belt of pastry around each olive. Place on an ungreased baking sheet.
- Bake for 20 minutes, or until golden brown.

Nutrition Information

- Calories: 230 calories
- Total Fat: 16.2 g
- Cholesterol: 0 mg
- Sodium: 265 mg
- Total Carbohydrate: 18.3 g
- Protein: 3 g

Parmesan and Parsley Sausage Ball Appetizer

"Biscuit mix, pork sausage, Cheddar, Parmesan and parsley are mixed together to make these savory and crowd-pleasing sausage balls."

Serving: 10 | Prep: 15 m | Cook: 25 m | Ready in: 40 m

Ingredients

- 3 cups biscuit baking mix
- 1 pound bulk pork sausage
- 4 cups shredded Cheddar cheese
- 1/2 cup grated Parmesan cheese
- 1/2 cup milk
- 1 1/2 teaspoons dried parsley

Direction

- Preheat an oven to 350 degrees F (175 degrees C). Grease a broiler pan or other pan with rack.
- Mix together the baking mix, sausage, Cheddar cheese, Parmesan cheese, milk, and parsley. Shape the mix into 1-inch balls and place on the prepared pan.
- Bake the sausage balls in the preheated oven until brown, about 25 minutes.

Nutrition Information

- Calories: 468 calories
- Total Fat: 31.6 g
- Cholesterol: 78 mg
- Sodium: 1206 mg
- Total Carbohydrate: 23.9 g

- Protein: 21.9 g

Parmesan Baskets

"Useful for holding other small snacks or appetizers. Can be made larger by increasing the size of the cheese mound and making the circle larger."

Serving: 24 | Prep: 10 m | Cook: 5 m | Ready in: 15 m

Ingredients

- 8 ounces freshly grated Parmesan cheese, divided

Direction

- Preheat oven to 350 degrees F (175 degrees C).
- Place about 2 teaspoons of Parmesan cheese onto a silicone sheet or baking sheet lined with parchment paper, and gently spread the cheese out into a circle about 2 inches in diameter. Spread more circles of cheese onto the baking sheet, keeping them at least 1 inch apart.
- Bake in the preheated oven until golden brown, 4 to 5 minutes. Watch carefully to avoid burning. Remove from the oven, and let cool on the sheets until warm; while still warm, drape the wafers over a small bowl or other container. Let cool. Store at room temperature in an airtight container.

Nutrition Information

- Calories: 39 calories
- Total Fat: 2.6 g
- Cholesterol: 7 mg
- Sodium: 161 mg
- Total Carbohydrate: 0.3 g

- Protein: 3.6 g

Pecan Snack

"These smell like a walk through a county fair, and they taste heavenly!"

Serving: 32 | Prep: 10 m | Cook: 1 h | Ready in: 1 h 10 m

Ingredients

- 1 egg white
- 1 tablespoon water
- 1 pound pecans
- 3/4 cup white sugar
- 1 teaspoon ground cinnamon
- 1 teaspoon salt

Direction

- Preheat oven to 250 degrees F (120 degrees C).
- In a large bowl, beat egg white with water until frothy. Stir in pecans and mix to coat. Combine sugar, cinnamon and salt and stir into pecan mixture. Spread on a baking sheet.
- Bake in preheated oven 1 hour, stirring every 15 minutes. Store in an airtight container.

Nutrition Information

- Calories: 117 calories
- Total Fat: 10.2 g
- Cholesterol: 0 mg
- Sodium: 74 mg
- Total Carbohydrate: 6.7 g
- Protein: 1.4 g

Peppered Pecans

"I like this roasted nut recipe because it doesn't use any added oil or butter - my husband likes this because it's nice and spicy! These have become a Thanksgiving tradition at our house, and make a tasty (albeit unusual) addition to salads, especially with the Maple Balsamic Vinaigrette from this site."

Serving: 20 | Prep: 15 m | Cook: 20 m | Ready in: 35 m

Ingredients

- 1 teaspoon finely ground black pepper
- 1 teaspoon ground white pepper
- 1 teaspoon ground cayenne pepper
- 1/2 teaspoon ground paprika
- 1/2 teaspoon ground dried thyme
- 2 egg whites
- 1 tablespoon Worcestershire sauce
- 1 teaspoon hot pepper sauce (such as Tabasco®)
- 1/8 teaspoon liquid smoke flavoring (optional)
- 1 pound pecan halves

Direction

- Preheat an oven to 375 degrees F (190 degrees C). Spray a large heavy roasting pan with cooking spray.
- Mix black pepper, white pepper, cayenne pepper, paprika, and dried thyme in a small bowl. Set aside.
- Whisk egg whites in a large bowl until foamy. Add Worcestershire, hot sauce, and liquid smoke flavoring and whisk to mix. Drop in pecans and stir to coat well. Pour coated pecans into a colander to drain off extra egg white

mixture; return to bowl and add the pepper mixture. Stir well to coat each pecan with spices.
- Spread pecans in prepared roasting pan. Roast in preheated oven for 5 minutes and stir pecans; roast an additional 5 minutes and stir again. Turn off heat and roast pecans an additional 5 to 10 minutes until pecans are lightly browned and fragrant. Let cool and serve at room temperature.

Nutrition Information

- Calories: 161 calories
- Total Fat: 16.4 g
- Cholesterol: 0 mg
- Sodium: 20 mg
- Total Carbohydrate: 3.6 g
- Protein: 2.5 g

Perfect Deviled Eggs

"These appeared on the table at every holiday and every gathering when I was growing up. My children will stand in front of the refrigerator and eat one after another (if I don't catch them). You can spice these up with country or creole mustard, a few jots of hot sauce (or a bunch of hot sauce!), and a sprig of parsley. It's just pretty."

Serving: 8 | Prep: 10 m | Cook: 20 m | Ready in: 1 h

Ingredients

- 8 eggs
- 1/3 cup mayonnaise
- 2 tablespoons Worcestershire sauce
- 2 tablespoons cream-style horseradish sauce
- 1 drop hot pepper sauce, or to taste
- salt and pepper to taste
- 1 teaspoon dried parsley flakes, for garnish
- 1 teaspoon paprika, for garnish

Direction

- Place the eggs into a saucepan in a single layer and fill with water to cover the eggs by 1 inch. Cover the saucepan and bring the water to a boil; remove from the heat and let the eggs stand in the hot water for 15 minutes. Drain the hot water and cool the eggs under cold running water in the sink; peel the cooled eggs.
- Cut the chilled eggs in half lengthwise. Place the yolks into a mixing bowl and set the whites aside. Mash the yolks with a fork until smooth; stir in the mayonnaise, Worcestershire sauce, horseradish sauce, hot sauce, salt, and pepper. Spoon

the yolk mixture into a heavy plastic bag; snip a corner off the bag to create a 1/2-inch opening. Pipe the yolks into the egg white halves. Sprinkle with parsley and paprika to garnish.

Nutrition Information

- Calories: 149 calories
- Total Fat: 13 g
- Cholesterol: 191 mg
- Sodium: 189 mg
- Total Carbohydrate: 1.8 g
- Protein: 6.5 g

Pickled Eggs III

"Use this recipe as a last minute side dish. These lightly spiced pickled eggs are always a treat, especially served with breads and cheeses."

Serving: 12 | Prep: 15 m | Cook: 40 m | Ready in: 2 d s55 m

Ingredients

- 12 eggs
- 1 cup tarragon vinegar
- 1 cup water
- 2 tablespoons white sugar
- 1 teaspoon salt
- 1/2 teaspoon celery seed
- 1 clove garlic, minced
- 2 bay leaves

Direction

- Place eggs in a large saucepan and cover with cold water. Bring water to a boil and immediately remove from heat. Cover and let eggs stand in hot water for 10 to 12 minutes. Remove from hot water, cool and peel.
- In a medium saucepan over medium heat, mix the tarragon vinegar, water, sugar, salt, celery seed, garlic and bay leaves. Bring to a boil, then simmer 30 minutes. Set aside to cool.
- Pour mixture over eggs; cover and refrigerate for 2 to 3 days.

Nutrition Information

- Calories: 80 calories
- Total Fat: 5 g

- Cholesterol: 186 mg
- Sodium: 264 mg
- Total Carbohydrate: 2.6 g
- Protein: 6.3 g

Pine Cone Cheese Ball

"Any cheese ball is a welcome addition to a holiday party spread, but when you bring one that looks like a pine cone, you're talking about a real showstopper."

Serving: 16 | Prep: 30 m | Ready in: 30 m

Ingredients

- 2 (8 ounce) packages cream cheese, softened
- 4 ounces goat cheese, softened
- 3 tablespoons chopped fresh flat-leaf parsley
- 2 tablespoons chopped fresh tarragon
- 1 tablespoon chopped fresh thyme
- 1/2 clove garlic, minced, or more to taste
- 1 pinch cayenne pepper, or to taste
- salt and ground black pepper to taste
- 1 cup whole almonds, or as needed
- 3 large fresh rosemary sprigs

Direction

- Stir cream cheese, goat cheese, parsley, tarragon, thyme, garlic, cayenne pepper, salt, and black pepper together in a bowl until smooth and well-mixed.
- Turn cheese mixture out onto a serving platter and form into a tapered oval shape to resemble a pine cone.
- Starting at the tapered end, press almonds into the cheese cone so that the tip of the almond is facing out and down, and cheese cone is completely covered with almonds and resembles a pine cone. Place rosemary sprigs at the top to resemble pine needles.

Nutrition Information

- Calories: 176 calories
- Total Fat: 16.4 g
- Cholesterol: 36 mg
- Sodium: 130 mg
- Total Carbohydrate: 2.9 g
- Protein: 5.6 g

Pumpkin Dip

"An excellent appetizer for the holidays! Serve with ginger snaps. MMMMM!"

Serving: 32 | Prep: 15 m | Ready in: 15 m

Ingredients

- 1 (8 ounce) package cream cheese, softened
- 2 cups confectioners' sugar
- 1 (15 ounce) can solid pack pumpkin
- 1 tablespoon ground cinnamon
- 1 tablespoon pumpkin pie spice
- 1 teaspoon frozen orange juice concentrate

Direction

- In a medium bowl, blend cream cheese and confectioners' sugar until smooth. Gradually mix in the pumpkin. Stir in the cinnamon, pumpkin pie spice, and orange juice until smooth and well blended. Chill until serving.

Nutrition Information

- Calories: 61 calories
- Total Fat: 2.5 g
- Cholesterol: 8 mg
- Sodium: 53 mg
- Total Carbohydrate: 9.4 g
- Protein: 0.7 g

Pumpkin Peanut Dip

"Sweet with a hint of pumpkin. Pairs great with sliced apples, pretzels, or crackers. Great for Halloween, a fall dinner party, or Thanksgiving."

Serving: 15 | Prep: 10 m | Cook: 5 m | Ready in: 1 h 15 m

Ingredients

- 1/2 (10.5 ounce) package miniature marshmallows
- 1 (8 ounce) package cream cheese, softened
- 1/4 cup sour cream
- 1/4 cup canned pumpkin
- 2 tablespoons peanut butter

Direction

- Place marshmallows in a saucepan over medium heat; cook and stir until marshmallows are melted, 3 to 5 minutes.
- Stir cream cheese, sour cream, pumpkin, and peanut butter together in a bowl. Beat marshmallows into the cream cheese mixture using an electric hand mixer until creamy. Chill in refrigerator 1 hour to allow flavors to blend.

Nutrition Information

- Calories: 110 calories
- Total Fat: 7.1 g
- Cholesterol: 18 mg
- Sodium: 69 mg
- Total Carbohydrate: 9.5 g
- Protein: 1.9 g

RanchStyle Deviled Eggs

"This is a basic deviled egg with a little twist of ranch."

Serving: 12 | Prep: 15 m | Cook: 15 m | Ready in: 1 h 30 m

Ingredients

- 6 eggs
- 1/4 cup mayonnaise
- 1 teaspoon ground black pepper
- 1 teaspoon ranch dressing mix
- 1 teaspoon prepared yellow mustard
- 1 pinch paprika, for garnish (optional)

Direction

- Place eggs in a saucepan and cover with cold water. Bring water to a boil and immediately remove from heat. Cover and let eggs stand in hot water for 10 to 12 minutes. Remove from hot water, cool and peel.
- Cut the eggs in half lengthwise and carefully remove the yolks to a bowl. Mash the yolks with the mayonnaise and mustard and season with pepper and ranch dressing mix, blending until smooth. Spoon the mixture into the egg white halves and garnish with a sprinkle of paprika.

Nutrition Information

- Calories: 70 calories
- Total Fat: 6.1 g
- Cholesterol: 95 mg
- Sodium: 75 mg
- Total Carbohydrate: 0.6 g
- Protein: 3.2 g

Rosemary and Brown Sugar Mixed Nuts

"This is a great upscale version of the same ol' bar nuts that you get served at every bar. This is a great party food. You can make these ahead of time. Just spread back out on wax paper until they are cooled and place back in to mixed nut jar."

Serving: 10 | Prep: 10 m | Cook: 10 m | Ready in: 20 m

Ingredients

- 1 (8.5 ounce) package mixed nuts
- 2 tablespoons dried rosemary
- 2 tablespoons kosher salt
- 2 tablespoons butter, melted
- 1/2 cup brown sugar

Direction

- Preheat an oven to 350 degrees F (175 degrees C). Line a baking sheet with waxed paper.
- Spread the mixed nuts into a single layer on the lined baking sheet.
- Roast the nuts in the preheated oven for 10 minutes.
- Sprinkle the rosemary and salt over the roasted nuts. Mix the butter and brown sugar together in a large bowl; add the nuts and toss to coat evenly. Spread the nuts again into an even layer on the lined baking sheet to serve.

Nutrition Information

- Calories: 207 calories
- Total Fat: 14.8 g
- Cholesterol: 6 mg

- Sodium: 1333 mg
- Total Carbohydrate: 17.3 g
- Protein: 4.2 g

Rosemary Sage Squash Seeds

"Perfect for eating on the go, a small snack, or even as a movie night popcorn replacement. Be sure to store any leftovers in an airtight bag or small container, which will keep them crispy for a few days after baking."

Serving: 2 | Prep: 10 m | Cook: 30 m | Ready in: 40 m

Ingredients

- 1/2 cup squash seeds
- 1 tablespoon olive oil
- 1 teaspoon dried rosemary, or more to taste
- 1/2 teaspoon salt
- 1/4 teaspoon dried sage

Direction

- Preheat oven to 300 degrees F (150 degrees C). Line a baking sheet with aluminum foil or parchment paper.
- Separate squash seeds from squash flesh, rinse through a fine-mesh strainer, and spread onto a paper towel to dry.
- Combine squash seeds, olive oil, rosemary, salt, and sage in a bowl and mix well. Spread seasoned seeds in a single layer onto the prepared baking sheet.
- Bake in the preheated oven, flipping every 10 minutes, until seeds are crunchy, 30 to 40 minutes.

Nutrition Information

- Calories: 248 calories
- Total Fat: 22.7 g
- Cholesterol: 0 mg

- Sodium: 588 mg
- Total Carbohydrate: 6.5 g
- Protein: 8.5 g

Sausage Stuffed Mushrooms

"This Johnsonvillle recipe is a must for mushroom fans! The taste of Johnsonville Italian Sausage pairs well with cream cheese, Parmesan cheese, lemon and garlic to create a dish that's bound to please! These stuffed mushrooms are perfect for an appetizer when you're entertaining family and friends."

Serving: 48 | Prep: 40 m | Cook: 16 m | Ready in: 56 m

Ingredients

- 1 (16 ounce) package Johnsonville® Ground Italian Sausage
- 48 large fresh mushrooms
- 1/2 cup dry bread crumbs
- 1 (8 ounce) package cream cheese, softened
- 3 garlic cloves, minced
- 2 tablespoons finely chopped fresh parsley
- 1 tablespoon lemon juice
- 1/4 cup grated Parmesan cheese

Direction

- In a skillet, cook and crumble sausage over medium heat until no longer pink and lightly browned; drain.
- Remove and discard stems from mushrooms. Arrange mushroom caps on foil-lined baking sheets.
- In a bowl, combine cooked sausage, bread crumbs, cream cheese, garlic, parsley and lemon juice. Stir until blended.
- Carefully spoon sausage mixture into mushroom caps. Sprinkle with cheese. Bake, uncovered, at 400 degrees F or until mushrooms are tender and lightly browned, Serve hot.

Nutrition Information

- Calories: 60 calories
- Total Fat: 4.7 g
- Cholesterol: 13 mg
- Sodium: 119 mg
- Total Carbohydrate: 1.9 g
- Protein: 2.9 g

Sausage Stuffing Balls

"This baked sausage ball recipe was given to me by my cousin. They are appetizers, but they also make great meatballs."

Serving: 20 | Prep: 20 m | Cook: 40 m | Ready in: 1 h

Ingredients

- 1/2 cup herb-seasoned dry bread stuffing mix
- 3/4 cup hot water
- 1 pound ground pork sausage
- 1/2 cup finely chopped onion
- 1/2 cup finely chopped celery
- 1 egg, beaten
- 1/2 teaspoon baking powder

Direction

- Preheat oven to 325 degrees F (165 degrees C).
- In a medium bowl, mix herb-seasoned dry bread stuffing mix with hot water. Gradually mix in pork until blended with the stuffing mix. Stir in onion, celery, egg and baking powder.
- Shape the mixture into 1 inch balls. Place the balls on a large baking sheet, cover with foil and bake in the preheated oven 15 minutes.
- Remove foil. Raise oven temperature to 350 degrees F (175 degrees C). Continue baking 25 minutes, until golden brown.

Nutrition Information

- Calories: 120 calories
- Total Fat: 9.6 g
- Cholesterol: 25 mg

- Sodium: 246 mg
- Total Carbohydrate: 4.6 g
- Protein: 3.6 g

Savory Pumpkin Hummus

"I tinkered a bit with what I found in other recipes and this is the result. I think I like my results. I stirred in a small handful of tamari-flavored pumpkin seeds just before serving (couldn't find plain ones) and sprinkled a bit of paprika on top to make it look nice."

Serving: 16 | Prep: 15 m | Ready in: 2 h 15 m

Ingredients

- 2 tablespoons lemon juice
- 2 tablespoons tahini
- 3 cloves garlic
- 3/4 teaspoon salt
- 2 (15 ounce) cans garbanzo beans, drained
- 2 teaspoons extra-virgin olive oil
- 1 (15 ounce) can pumpkin puree
- 1 teaspoon ground cumin
- 1/2 teaspoon cayenne pepper
- 1/4 cup toasted pumpkin seed kernels, or more to taste
- 1 pinch paprika

Direction

- Pulse lemon juice, tahini, garlic, and salt together in a food processor or blender until smooth. Add garbanzo beans and olive oil and pulse until smooth. Add pumpkin, cumin, and cayenne pepper; process until well blended. Transfer hummus to a container with a lid and refrigerate at least 2 hours.
- Fold pumpkin seeds into hummus; garnish with paprika.

Nutrition Information

- Calories: 81 calories
- Total Fat: 3.1 g
- Cholesterol: 0 mg
- Sodium: 281 mg
- Total Carbohydrate: 11.3 g
- Protein: 3 g

Seasoned Crackers

"These crackers are a quick and easy party snack or could even be used as a garnish for a cup of chowder."

Serving: 12 | Prep: 10 m | Cook: 20 m | Ready in: 30 m

Ingredients

- 1 (12 ounce) package oyster crackers
- 1 (1 ounce) package ranch dressing mix
- 1/2 teaspoon dried dill weed
- 1/4 teaspoon garlic powder
- 3/4 cup vegetable oil

Direction

- Preheat oven to 200 degrees F (95 degrees C).
- Whisk together the oil and seasonings; add crackers and toss to coat evenly.
- Spread evenly on large baking sheet and bake for 20 minutes. Stir after 10 minutes and continue baking 10 minutes more.

Nutrition Information

- Calories: 256 calories
- Total Fat: 18.8 g
- Cholesterol: 0 mg
- Sodium: 699 mg
- Total Carbohydrate: 19.4 g
- Protein: 2.3 g

Serious Herb Cheese Spread

"Served on crackers, this savory cheese spread is perfect for whetting the appetite before the big dinner."

Serving: 16 | Prep: 15 m | Ready in: 2 h 15 m

Ingredients

- 1 (8 ounce) package cream cheese, softened
- 2 cloves garlic, minced
- 1/2 teaspoon prepared mustard
- 1/2 teaspoon Worcestershire sauce
- 1/4 cup chopped parsley
- 1/4 cup chopped fresh dill weed
- 1/4 cup chopped fresh basil
- 1/4 cup chopped black olives
- 1 1/2 tablespoons lemon juice

Direction

- In a medium bowl, mix cream cheese, garlic, mustard, Worcestershire sauce, parsley, dill weed, basil, olives and lemon juice. Transfer to desired mold, and chill in the refrigerator at least 2 hours before serving.

Nutrition Information

- Calories: 53 calories
- Total Fat: 5.1 g
- Cholesterol: 15 mg
- Sodium: 63 mg
- Total Carbohydrate: 0.9 g

- Protein: 1.2 g

Shrimp Cheese Ball

"A great party treat."

Serving: 12 | Prep: 20 m | Cook: 10 m | Ready in: 3 h

Ingredients

- 1 cup butter
- 1/2 cup minced garlic
- 1 small red onion, chopped
- 1 tablespoon Cajun seasoning
- 1 tablespoon cayenne pepper
- 1 tablespoon crushed red pepper flakes
- 1 pound uncooked shrimp, peeled and cut into pieces
- 1 1/2 (8 ounce) packages cream cheese, softened
- 1 teaspoon liquid smoke flavoring
- 1 teaspoon lemon juice
- 1/2 cup chopped pecans
- 1 bunch fresh parsley, chopped
- 1/2 cup chopped pecans

Direction

- Melt the butter in a large skillet over medium heat. Stir in the garlic, onion, Cajun seasoning, cayenne pepper, and red pepper flakes; cook and stir until the onion has softened and turned translucent, about 5 minutes. Stir in the shrimp. Cook the shrimp until they are bright pink on the outside and the meat is no longer transparent in the center, about 5 minutes. Drain and discard any excess grease. Set aside.
- Mix cream cheese, liquid smoke, and lemon juice in a large bowl. Stir in the shrimp and 1/2 cup of pecans, mixing until evenly distributed. Roll the mixture into a ball. Cover with

plastic wrap and refrigerate until slightly firm, about 30 minutes. Mix the parsley with the remaining 1/2 cup of pecans in a bowl. Roll the cheese ball in the parsley mixture until the ball is covered. Cover and refrigerate the cheese ball until completely firm, about 2 hours.

Nutrition Information

- Calories: 358 calories
- Total Fat: 33 g
- Cholesterol: 129 mg
- Sodium: 371 mg
- Total Carbohydrate: 6.1 g
- Protein: 11.6 g

Shrimp Dip

"My mom serves this appetizer every Thanksgiving with fresh cut carrots, cauliflower, celery, and red peppers!"

Serving: 32

Ingredients

- 3 pounds cooked salad shrimp
- 6 (8 ounce) packages cream cheese
- 1 pint sour cream
- 1 (12 fluid ounce) can or bottle chile sauce

Direction

- In a mixing bowl, blend together the shrimp, cream cheese, sour cream and chili sauce. Season to taste with salt and ground pepper, serve with favorite crackers.

Nutrition Information

- Calories: 224 calories
- Total Fat: 18.1 g
- Cholesterol: 136 mg
- Sodium: 227 mg
- Total Carbohydrate: 2.7 g
- Protein: 12.8 g

Simple Deviled Eggs

"The eggs are delicious, and it's easy to make more for larger gatherings. I've added onion and celery for a little more flavor and texture."

Serving: 2 | Prep: 15 m | Ready in: 15 m

Ingredients

- 6 hard-cooked eggs
- 2 tablespoons mayonnaise
- 1 teaspoon white sugar
- 1 teaspoon white vinegar
- 1 teaspoon prepared mustard
- 1/2 teaspoon salt
- 1 tablespoon finely chopped onion
- 1 tablespoon finely chopped celery
- 1 pinch paprika, or to taste

Direction

- Slice eggs in half lengthwise and remove yolks; set whites aside. Mash yolks with a fork in a small bowl. Stir in mayonnaise, sugar, vinegar, mustard, salt, onion, and celery; mix well. Stuff or pipe egg yolk mixture into egg whites. Sprinkle with paprika. Refrigerate until serving.

Nutrition Information

- Calories: 327 calories
- Total Fat: 26 g
- Cholesterol: 563 mg
- Sodium: 902 mg

- Total Carbohydrate: 4.7 g
- Protein: 19.3 g

Part 2

Introduction

I create cooking book that comes along with Thanksgiving and the holiday season. This book is here with easy recipes for you. If you're a food lover or love cooking, this book best for you!

Includes delicious breakfast recipes, Thanksgiving sides that will make your turkey jealous, main dishes like turkey and ham, desserts.

Choose a few of your favorite recipes and spend time with your family.

Be thankful for the moments you get together. Happy cooking!

Cider roasted chicken

prep time 20 mins
prepare time one hour 20 mins
total time one hour 40 mins
servings 6 servings

INGREDIENTS
- half cup raw walnuts
- 2 tablespoons honey
- 8 ounces goat cheese softened
- 2 tablespoons fresh sage chopped
- 2 teaspoons fresh rosemary chopped
- 2 tablespoons olive oil
- salt and pepper to taste
- 1 pound whole chicken 4-5
- 1 cloves head of garlic bottom sliced off to reveal the
- 2 apples quartered
- 4 tablespoons butter
- 1 half pounds fresh red grapes
- 3 cups apple cider

INSTRUCTIONS
1. Preheat the oven to 425 degrees F.

2. Place a small skilallow over medium heat. Place the walnuts + honey and prepare till toasted and caramelized, about 5 mins. Take away the walnuts from the skilallow and deploy out on a plate in a single layer. Allow to cool down and then delicately chop the walnuts.
3. In a small bowl, blend along the goat cheese, chopped walnuts, sage and rosemary.
4. Take away the chicken giblets. Rinse the chicken inside and out. Pat the outside dry. Generously salt and pepper the inside of the chicken. Stuff the cavity with the garlic and 1 quartered apple. Slide your hand between the meat and skin of the chicken and then attentively stuff the goat cheese mixture under the skin, pushing it as far back as you'll get it without actually ripping the skin. Depending on the size of your chicken, you may not employ all the goat cheese. If this is the case, simply strew the goat cheese around the grapes before roasting.
5. Rub the chicken all over with olive oil and then strew generously with salt + pepper. Tie the legs along with kitchen string and tuck the wing tips under the body of the chicken.
6. Place the grapes and remaining apples in a roasting pan or big cast iron skillet. Drizzle with salt, pepper and olive oil. Place a few fresh sage leaves and any remaining goat cheese.
7. Place chicken onto the grapes. Place four tablespoon size pats of butter around the chicken.
8. Roast the chicken for 1 to one hour 15 mins, or till the juices run clear just as you cut between a leg and thigh. Place the cider to a medium size pot and bring to a seethe, reduce the heat and simmer till it thickens and is reduced by about half. Halfway through cooking the chicken, brush the bird with half of the cider. About 5 mins before the chicken is done cooking, brush it again with the remaining cider. If desired, you'll also resubmit some cider for serving.
9. Allow the chicken to sit for ten-20 mins, covered with foil and then slice and service!

Smoky pumpkin beer and potato soup

prep time 20 mins
prepare time 30 mins
total time 50 mins
servings 6 servings

INGREDIENTS
- 4 tablespoons butter
- 1 small sweet onion diced
- 1 potato peeled + diced
- 2 cloves garlic minced or grated
- One-quarter cup flour
- 2 cups of your favorite pumpkin beer
- 2 One-quarter cups low sodium chicken broth
- 2 cups pumpkin puree*
- 1-2 in chipotle chilies adobo minced
- 2 teaspoons fresh thyme
- half teaspoon smoked paprika

- half teaspoon curry powder
- salt + pepper to taste
- one cup heavy cream or whole milk
- one cup smoked gouda shredded
- one cup smoked cheddar shredded

POPCORN
- 4 slices thick cut smoked bacon, chopped
- half cup pepitas shelled pumpkin seeds
- 2 tablespoons refined sugar
- 4-5 cups air or stove popped popcorn
- salt to taste

INSTRUCTIONS

1. Heat a big soup pot over medium heat, place the butter to melt. Once melted, place the onion and prepare till it begins to caramelize, about 8 mins. Place the potato + garlic and continue cooking another 5 mins or till the potato is tender. Strew the flour over the veggies and prepare 1 minute, stirring the flour around so it coats the veggies. Spice gently with salt + pepper.
2. Slowly Rain within the beer + broth, add often to avoid any clumps from forming. Add within the pumpkin puree, chipotle chiles, thyme, smoked paprika and curry powder. Bring the soup to a seethe and then reduce the heat to a simmer. Simmer 15 mins or till the potato is completely soft. If desired, Place the soup to a blender and puree till completely sleek.
3. Add within the heavy cream, smoked gouda and smoked cheddar, prepare over low heat till the cheese is fully melted. If the soup is too thick for your liking, thin with more chicken broth.
4. Share the soup among bowls and over with popcorn and more cheese if desired. Enjoy!

POPCORN

1. Preheat the oven to 350 degrees F. Align a baking sheet with foil.
2. Deploy the bacon and pepitas out on the baking sheet and blend well with the refined sugar. Deploy them into an even layer.
3. Bake for ten mins and then take away from the oven and place the popcorn, blend the mixture along very well, making sure the bacon lubricates and refined sugar coat the popcorn. If the mixture seems dry, place 1 tablespoon butter or olive oil. Place back within the oven and continue baking another ten-15 mins, tossing once throughout cooking till the bacon is crisp. Keep in mind that the bacon can crisp up a bit more once it's out of the oven. Take away from the oven and submit aover the soup!

Harvest cranberry, burrata salad

prep time ten mins
prepare time 5 mins
total time 15 mins
servings 6 servings

INGREDIENTS
- half cup raw walnuts
- half cup pepitas
- 2 tablespoon maple syrup
- flaky sea salt
- 3-4 cups baby kale and or arugula
- 3-4 fuyu persimmons cored + cut into wedges
- 2 clementines peeled
- three-quarters cups dried cranberries
- 8 ounces fresh burrata cheese torn

CRANBERRY BALSAMIC DRESSING
- One-quarter cup ten0% cranberry or pomegranate juice
- One-quarter cup balsamic vinegar

- 1 tablespoon lemon juice
- one-third cup olive oil
- salt + pepper to taste

INSTRUCTIONS

1. Mix the walnuts, pepitas and maple syrup in a medium size skillet. Place the skilallow over medium heat and prepare for 5-6 mins or till the mixture becomes golden, toasted and caramelized. Take away the nuts and seeds from the skilallow and Place to a plate. Strew with salt and allow cool.
2. In a big bowl or on a big serving plate, mix the greens, persimmons, clementines and cranberries. Place the torn Burrata cheese and strew on the walnuts and pepitas.
3. In a small bowl, blend along the ingredients for the dressing. Try and adsimply salt + pepper to your liking. Drizzle the dressing over the salad or submit along side the salad. EAT

Skilallow cranberry roasted

<u>15 mins</u>
prepare time 45 mins
total time one hour

<u>servings 4</u>

INGREDIENTS

- 4 skin-on chicken breasts or thighs
- One-quarter cup olive oil divided
- 1 tablespoon chopped fresh thyme
- 1 half teaspoons chopped fresh rosemary
- 2 cloves garlic minced or grated
- zest + juice of half lemon
- kosher salt and pepper
- 1 pound baby potatoes halved
- 3 carrots chopped
- one cup white wine or chicken broth
- 1 half cups fresh cranberries
- 2 tablespoons refined sugar
- 2 tablespoons balsamic

INSTRUCTIONS

1. Preheat the oven to 425 degrees F.
2. Rub the chicken with 2 tablespoons olive oil, the thyme, rosemary, garlic and lemon zest. Spice with salt and pepper.
3. Heat a big oven safe skilallow over medium-high heat. Place 2 tablespoons olive oil. Just as the oil shimmers, place the chicken, skin side down, and sear till golden, about 5 mins. Flip and prepare 5 mins more. Take away the chicken from the skillet. Place 2 tablespoons butter, the potatoes, carrots, and a pinch every of salt and pepper. Cook, stirring often, till sgently softened, about 5 mins. Rain within the wine, deglazing the pan and scraping up any browned bits off the bottom. Simmer the wine for 5 mins or till reduced sgently. Take away from the heat and nestle the chicken into the potatoes. Place the lemon juice.
4. In a small bowl, blend along the cranberries, refined sugar and balsamic vinegar. Strew the cranberries over the chicken. Place to the oven and roast for 20-25 mins or till the chicken is prepared through and the potatoes are tender.

Plate the chicken and potatoes and drizzle with the sauce left within the pan. EAT!

Crockpot beef chili

prep time 15 mins
prepare time 6 hours
total time 6 hours 15 mins
servings 8

INGREDIENTS
- 1 tablespoon olive oil
- 2 small onions, chopped
- 4 cloves garlic, minced or grated
- 2 pounds lean ground beef
- 2 poblano peppers, seeded and chopped
- 1 tablespoon chili powder
- 1 tablespoon smoked paprika
- 2 teaspoons ground cumin
- 1 half teaspoons ground cinnamon

- 1 half teaspoons salt
- half teaspoon cayenne
- 2-3 cups low sodium chicken broth
- 1 (28 ounce) can crushed tomatoes
- 1 (8 ounce) can tomato paste
- 2 tablespoons maple syrup
- 2 leaves bay
- cheddar cheese, avocado, green onions and cilantro, for serving

INSTRUCTIONS

1. Heat a big skilallow over medium heat and place the olive oil. Place the onion and prepare about 5 mins or till it begins to caramelize around the edges. Add the garlic and prepare another minute. Employ your hands to crumble the ground beef into the pot. Brown the beef, breaking up the meat as you go, about 8 mins. Once the beef is browned, place within the poblano pepper, chili powder, smoked paprika, cumin, cinnamon, salt and cayenne. Give it a good add and allow prepare about a minute or two. Take away the skilallow from the heat.
2. Place the beef mixture to the bowl of your crockpot. Place 2 cups chicken broth, the tomatoes, tomato paste, maple, and bay leaves, add to mix. Overlay and prepare on low for 6-8 hours or hight for 4-5 hours. If your chili is too thick, place the remaining broth to thin.
3. Take away the bay leaves and ladle the chili into bowls. Over with cheddar cheese, avocado and fresh cilantro. Eat!

Fall harvest quinoa salad

prep time 15 mins
prepare time 30 mins
total time 45 mins
servings 6

INGREDIENTS
- one cup unprepared quinoa
- 1 delicata or acorn squash halved, seeded + cut into half circles
- 2 tablespoons olive oil
- 2 tablespoons maple syrup
- half teaspoon McCormick Ground Cinnamon
- pinch of McCormick Ground Cayenne Red Pepper to taste
- kosher salt + pepper
- 1 half cups baby kale
- 1 apple cored + thinly sliced
- arils from 1 pomegranate

- One-quarter cup toasted pumpkin seeds or roasted pistachios
- 8 ounces' halloumi cheese sliced (omit if vegan)
- 1 avocado sliced

TURMERIC TAHINI DRESSING
- One-quarter cup tahini
- 2 tablespoons lemon juice
- 1 tablespoon apple cider vinegar
- 2 tablespoons olive oil
- half teaspoon [McCormick Ground Turmeric
- kosher salt + pepper

INSTRUCTIONS
1. Prepare quinoa according to package directions.
2. Preheat the oven to 425 degrees F.
3. On a baking sheet, blend along the squash, olive oil, maple, cinnamon, cayenne and a good pinch of salt + pepper. Place within the oven and roast for 25-30 mins, tossing twice throughout cooking till the squash is tender and gently caramelized.
4. In a big bowl, mix the warm quinoa, roasted squash, kale, apples, pomegranate arils and pumpkin seeds. Gently blend to mix.
5. Heat a medium skilallow over medium heat and place a drizzle of olive oil. Once hot, place the Halloumi slices and prepare for 1-2 mins per side or till gently golden. Take away and drain on to paper towels.
6. Over the quinoa with the fried Halloumi and avocado and drizzle with the turmeric tahini dressing. Garnish with a handful of pomegranate arils if desired. Submit warm or at about 25 °C.

TURMERIC TAHINI DRESSING
1. In a blender mix the tahini, turmeric, lemon juice, apple cider vinegar, turmeric, salt and pepper. Place 2 tablespoons water and blend till sleek, adding water to thwithin the

dressing till it is pourable. Try and adsimply salt + pepper to your liking.

Thanksgiving turkey hot dish

prep time ten mins
prepare time 30 mins
total time 40 mins
   servings 6

INGREDIENTS
- 4 croissants halved
- 4 tablespoons butter
- cup leftover turkey warmed (at least 1)
- cup leftover gravy warmed (at least 1)
- 1 half cups shredded sharp cheddar cheese
- 3 ounces prosciutto torn (optional)
- 2 cups tater tots
- leftover cranberry sauce
- fried sage for serving

INSTRUCTIONS

1. Preheat the oven to 375 degrees F. Lubricate a square baking dish or ten-inch skillet.
2. Align the croissants, cut side up, within the baking dish and place a small pat of butter on every. Place the turkey in an even layer and then drizzle the gravy overtop. Over with a layer of cheese and then place the prosciutto. Lay the tater tots in an even layer. Place to the oven and bake for 30-40 mins or till the tater tots are crisp. Service!

Roasted butternut persimmon salad

prep time 15 mins
prepare time 30 mins
total time 45 mins
    servings 6

INGREDIENTS
- 4 cups cubed butternut squash or a blend of butternut and delicata
- half cup plus 2 tablespoons olive oil
- 2 tablespoons maple syrup

- half teaspoon cinnamon
- One-quarter teaspoon ginger
- One-quarter teaspoon cayenne
- kosher salt and pepper
- half cup dried cranberries
- three-quarters cup apple cider
- 2 tablespoons apple cider vinegar
- 2 teaspoons dijon mustard
- 1-ounce log cut cheese sliced into One-quarter inch rounds, ten
- one-third cup buttermilk or 1 egg beaten
- one-third cup panka bread crumbs
- 6 cups mixed greens
- 3 persimmons quartered
- half cup toasted pecans

INSTRUCTIONS

1. Preheat the oven to 425 degrees F.
2. Deploy the butternut squash out in a single layer on a baking sheet. Drizzle 2 tablespoons olive oil, maple syrup, cinnamon, ginger, cayenne, salt and pepper, blend well to coat. Roast within the oven till the butternut squash is tender, 20 to 25 mins, stirring halfway through cooking. Take away from oven and add in cranberries.
3. Meanwhereas, heat the apple cider and the cider vinegar in a small saucepan over high heat and seethe till it has reduced to One-quarter cup, about 6-8 mins. Take away from the heat and blend within the remaining half cup olive oil and the mustard. Spice with salt and pepper.
4. To prepare the Fried Goat Cheese. Heat 2 tablespoons olive oil in a skilallow over medium heat.
5. Place the panko to one small bowl, then place the buttermilk to another small bowl. Attentively dip the rounds of goat cheese, first through the buttermilk, and then dredge through the panko. Attentively place to the hot skilallow and prepare for 2-3 mins per side or till golden. To prepare these

in advance, fry as directed and then warm in a 300-degree oven for 5 mins.
6. In a big salad bowl, blend along the lettuce, roasted squash, persimmons, and pecans. Place the dressing and blend once more. Over with the fried goat cheese. Enjoy warm or at about 25 °C.

RECIPE NOTES

<u>If you are short on time, skip frying the cheese and simply crumble the goat cheese over the salad.</u>

Pumpkin butter rugelach cookies

prep time 20 mins
prepare time 30 mins
total time 50 mins
    servings 48

INGREDIENTS

- 2 sticks (1 cup) unsalted butter, at about 25 °C
- 8 ounces' cream cheese, at about 25 °C
- 2 tablespoons granulated sugar
- 1 teaspoon vanilla extract
- One-quarter teaspoon kosher salt
- 2 cups all-purpose flour

PUMPKIN BUTTER

- 1 (15 ounce) can pumpkin puree
- one-third cup light refined sugar
- 2 tablespoons real maple syrup
- 1 teaspoon vanilla extract
- 1 teaspoon pumpkin pie spice

- half teaspoon cinnamon
- one cup pecans or walnuts, delicately chopped
- 1 egg, beaten
- coarse sugar, for sprinkling

INSTRUCTIONS

1. 1. In a big mixing bowl, cream along the butter, cream cheese, sugar, and vanilla till light and fluffy, 2-3 mins. Place the flour and salt, beating till mixd. The dough possibly wet.
- Heap the dough out onto a well floured counter and shape into a ball. Cut into 4 equal pieces. Overlay with plastic wrap and Chill 30 mins.
- Meanwhereas, prepare the pumpkin butter. In a medium sauce pan, mix the pumpkin, refined sugar, maple, pumpkin pie spice, and cinnamon. Bring to a gentle seethe over medium heat. Cook, stirring often till the pumpkin thickens sgently, however is unfoldable, about ten-20 mins. Allow cool (the pumpkin butter can thicken as it cools). Any leftovers possibly kept within the fridge for up to 2 weeks.
- On a well floured counter, roll every ball of dough out into a 9-inch circle. Deploy 2 tablespoons of pumpkin butter over the dough and then strew with One-quarter cup nuts. Gently Put the nuts into the dough. Cut the circle into 12 wedges (see above photo). Operating with the wide edge, roll the cookies up into a crescent and place on a parchment lined baking sheet. Recur with the remaining dough. Chill the cookies for 15 mins within the freezer or up to overnight within the fridge.
- Preheat the oven to 350 degrees F.
- Brush every cookie with the beaten egg and then strew with coarse sugar. Place to the oven and bake for 15-20 mins, till gently golden brown. Place to a wire rack to cool down completely or enjoy warm with a dusting of powdered sugar.

Caramelized garlic butter

prep time 15 mins
prepare time 30 mins
total time 45 mins
<u>servings ten</u>

INGREDIENTS
- 1 stick (half cup) salted butter
- 4-6 cloves garlic
- 2 teaspoons chopped fresh oregano
- half teaspoon crushed red pepper flakes
- 1 sourdough baguette, halved lengthwise and cut in 6 pieces
- one cup grated parmesan cheese
- 1 tablespoon extra virgin olive oil
- 1 pound mixed mushrooms
- 2 teaspoons chopped fresh thyme, plus more for serving
- kosher salt and pepper
- One-quarter cup white wine

- One-quarter cup buttermilk
- One-quarter cup heavy cream

INSTRUCTIONS

1. 1. Preheat the oven to 425 degrees F.
- In a big skillet, mix the butter, garlic, and oregano. Prepare over medium low heat, stirring often till the garlic is golden and caramelized, about 15 mins. The butter can brown sgently. Take away from the heat and delicately mash the garlic with a fork. Add within the crushed red pepper flakes.
- Lay the bread on a baking sheet. Drizzle/rub the garlic butter onto every cut side of bread. Over with cheese and Place to the oven for 8-ten mins or till the cheese has melted.
- Meanwhereas, comeback the skilallow to medium heat and place the olive oil. Just as the oil shimmers, place the mushrooms. Cooking, undistributed till the mushrooms are golden on the bottom, about 3-5 mins, add and place the thyme and a pinch every of salt and pepper. Reduce the heat to low, place the wine, buttermilk, and cream. Prepare till warmed though, about 5 mins. Take away from the heat and spice as needed with salt and pepper.
- Lay the garlic bread on a serving plate and spoon the mushrooms over top. Alternately, you'll submit the garlic bread alongside the mushrooms for dipping/spoon over the bread. Over with thyme. EAT!

Butternut squash

prep time 15 mins
prepare time 45 mins
total time one hour
    <u>servings 6</u>

INGREDIENTS
- 5 cups peeled, cubed butternut squash
- 3 cloves garlic, smashed
- 2 tablespoons extra virgin olive oil
- 2 tablespoons honey
- 1 tablespoon chopped fresh sage, plus more for serving
- half teaspoon smoked paprika
- half teaspoon cayenne pepper
- half teaspoon cinnamon
- kosher salt and pepper

- 2 cups whole milk
- 2 cups low sodium veggie or chicken broth
- 6-8 ounces brie, rind take awayd
- 2 tablespoons butter
- 4 ounces thinly sliced pancetta
- cream, for topping (optional)

INSTRUCTIONS

1. 1. Preheat the oven to 400 degrees F.
- In a big, oven safe soup pot, mix the butternut squash, garlic, olive oil, honey, sage, paprika, cayenne, cinnamon, and a pinch every of salt and pepper. Blend well to mix. Place to the oven and roast for 20-25 mins or till the squash is tender.
- Place the roasted veggies to a blender and place the broth, puree till sleek. Comeback the soup to the pot and set over medium heat on the stove. Place the milk. Bring the soup to a simmer over medium heat, add within the brie and butter till liquified and sleek. If needed, thwithin the soup with extra milk or broth. Try and adsimply seasonings as desired.
- Heat a small skilallow over medium heat. Place the pancetta and prepare till crisp, about 2 mins per side.
- Share the soup among bowls and over with crisp pancetta, sage, and a drizzle of cream, if desired. Enjoy!

Roasted squash, caramelized fig

prep time 15 mins
prepare time 30 mins
total time 45 mins
servings 4

INGREDIENTS
- 1 kabocha or acorn squash, sliced
- One-quarter cup + 2 tablespoons extra virgin olive oil
- One-quarter cup honey
- 2 tablespoons fresh thyme leaves
- kosher salt
- 16-20 fresh or dried figs, halved
- 2 tablespoons lemon juice
- 2 tablespoons apple cider vinegar
- 1 tablespoon orange zest
- black pepper

- 4 cups baby arugula
- 4 ounces feta cheese crumbles
- arils from 1 pomegranate

INSTRUCTIONS

1. 1. Preheat the oven to 425 degrees F.
- On a rimmed baking sheet, blend along the squash, 2 tablespoons olive oil, honey, 1 half tablespoons thyme leaves, and a good pinch of salt. Place to the oven and roast for 20 mins. Take away from the oven, place the figs to the baking sheet and blend to mix. Comeback to the oven and roast another ten-15 mins or till the figs have caramelized. If employing dried figs, prepare them only 5 mins. This can soften them.
- To prepare the dressing: In a mason jar, mix the remaining One-quarter cup olive oil, lemon juice, apple cider vinegar, remaining half tablespoon thyme, orange zest, and a pinch every of kosher salt and pepper.
- Place the arugula to a big salad bowl and over with the roasted squash and figs. Crumble the feta overover and strew with pomegranate arils. Drizzle with the dressing. Enjoy!

Brie stuffed crispy

prep time ten mins
prepare time 45 mins
total time 55 mins
<u>servings 8</u>

INGREDIENTS
- 1 half pounds mixed baby potatoes
- 1 tablespoon extra virgin olive oil
- kosher salt and pepper
- 3 tablespoons butter, melted
- 2 cloves garlic, grated
- 2 tablespoons chopped fresh thyme
- 8 ounces' brie, cut into small wedges
- 1-2 teaspoons white truffle oil
- 8 pan-fried sage leaves
- crushed pink peppercorn

INSTRUCTIONS

1. 1. Preheat the oven to 400 degrees F.
- On a big baking sheet, blend along the potatoes, olive oil and a pinch every of salt and pepper. Place to the oven and roast 20 mins or till the potatoes are fork tender. Employing a potato masher or a fork, gently Put down on the potatoes, smashing them to about One-quarter inch thickness.
- Blend along the butter, garlic, and thyme. Drizzle the butter over the potatoes and comeback the potatoes to the oven and roast another 20-25 mins or till golden and crisp. During the last 5 mins of cooking, place a thin slice of brie to every potato and roast till melted.
- Lay the warm potatoes on a serving plate and drizzle with truffle oil. Over with sage and peppercorns. Enjoy!

Cinnamon streemployl

prep time 15 mins
prepare time one hour

total time one hour 15 mins
servings 8

INGREDIENTS

- 4 medium sweet potatoes
- One-quarter cup real maple syrup
- 2 teaspoons vanilla extract
- 1 teaspoon ground cinnamon
- One-quarter cup heavy cream
- 4 tablespoons salted butter, melted
- 2 eggs, gently beaten

STREEMPLOYL

- half cup all-purpose flour
- half cup refined sugar, packed
- half cup real maple syrup
- one cup raw walnuts, delicately chopped
- 1 teaspoon cinnamon
- 8 tablespoons cold butter, cubed

INSTRUCTIONS

1. 1. Preheat your oven to 400 degrees F. Lubricate a 9x13 inch baking dish or a dish slighly smaller (no less than 2 quarts).
- Poke a few holes within the sweet potatoes and bake for one hour or till soft and tender. Just as the sweet potatoes are cooked, slice them in half and allow to cool down. Reduce the oven temperature to 350 degrees F.
- Peel the skins away from the sweet potatoes and mash well in a big mixing bowl. Blend within the maple syrup, vanilla, cinnamon, heavy cream, butter, and eggs, mixing till mixd.
- To prepare the streemployl. In a medium bowl, mix the flour, refined sugar and cinnamon. Place 6 tablespoons butter and employ your fingers to blend the butter into the flour till a crumble forms. Add in One-quarter cup maple syrup and the walnuts.

- Rain half the sweet potatoes into the pre readyd dish. Strew with one-third of the streemployl. Deploy the remaining sweet potatoes over over and strew the remaining streemployl evenly over the over of the sweet potatoes. Place to the oven and bake for 30-40 mins or till the over is dark golden.
- Meanwhereas, in a small sauce pan, brown the remaining 2 tablespoons butter over medium heat. Add within the remaining maple syrup.
- Simply before serving, drizzle the browned maple butter over the casserole. Submit warm.

Tomato white lasagna

prep time 30 mins
prepare time one hour 30 mins
total time two hours
servings 8

INGREDIENTS

- 4 cups butternut squash, cubed (about 1 medium squash)
- 2 tablespoons extra virgin olive oil
- 1 tablespoon honey
- kosher salt and pepper
- 6 tablespoons butter
- 2 cloves garlic, minced or grated
- 1 tablespoon fresh sage, chopped
- 1 tea spoon dried basil
- One-quarter cup flour
- 3 half cups whole milk
- One-quarter teaspoon fresh grated nutmeg
- one cup shredded fontina cheese
- one cup parmesan cheese, grated
- 2 cups whole milk ricotta
- 2 cups shredded provolone
- 1 jar (8 ounce) oil packed sun-dried tomatoes, oil drained and chopped
- 1 box no-seethe lasagna noodles
- 2 tablespoons toasted pine nuts

INSTRUCTIONS

1. 1. Heat up oven to 375 degrees F. Lubricate a 9x13 inch pan.
- On a baking sheet, blend along the butternut squash, olive oil, honey, and a pinch every of salt and pepper. Place to the oven and roast for 25-30 mins or till the squash is tender.
- Soften the butter in a medium sauce pan. Place the garlic, sage, and basil and prepare 30 seconds or till fragrant. Blend within the flour and prepare for about 1 minute. Slowly place the milk. Add within the nutmeg and spice with salt and pepper. Bring to a seethe and add for 1 minute. Remove from heat and add within the fontina cheese and half cup of parmesan cheese. Add till the

cheese is fully liquified and the sauce is sleek. Set the cheese sauce aside.
- In a medium bowl, mash the roasted butternut squash till mostly sleek. Add within the ricotta, provolone, and sun-dried tomatoes.
- Deploy One-quarter of the cheese sauce within the bottom of the pre readyd baking dish. Over with 3-4 lasagna sheets. Deploy with half the butternut squash mixture and then another One-quarter of the cheese sauce. Place another 3-4 lasagna noodles on top, and then over with the remaining butternut squash mixture and another One-quarter of the cheese sauce. Place the remaining lasagna noodles and Rain the remaining One-quarter of the cheese sauce over top. Over with the remaining half cup of parmesan cheese. Bake uncovered for 45 mins or till the over has bubbled up and browned a bit. Allow stand ten mins before serving. Over with pine nuts and fried sage.

Pistachio chocolate baklava

prep time 20 mins
prepare time 45 mins
total time one hour 5 mins
servings 8

INGREDIENTS

- 2 cups pistachios, roasted, salted, and roughly chopped
- one cup almonds, roasted or raw, and roughly chopped
- 1 half cups semi-sweet chocolate chips
- half teaspoon cinnamon
- 24 sheets frozen phyllo dough, thawed (about half a pound)
- 1 stick salted butter, melted
- one cup honey
- 2 teaspoons vanilla extract

INSTRUCTIONS

1. 1. Preheat the oven to 350 degrees F. Align a 9-inch spring form pan with parchment paper.
- In a medium bowl, mix the pistachios, almonds, chocolate chips, and cinnamon.
- Fold 1 sheet of phyllo dough in half and then place within the pre readyd pan. Brush the phyllo dough with liquified butter. Repeat, layering 8 more times, placing the sheets of dough over over of every other. Spoon half of the nut/chocolate blend over the dough. Now place another 8 sheets of phyllo, brushing every with butter. Spoon over the remaining filling. Place another 8 sheet of phyllo, agin brushing every with butter.
- Cut the baklava into 8 triangles. Place the pan on a baking sheet and Place to the oven and bake for 45-50 mins, till phyllo is golden brown.
- Meanwhereas, mix half cup water and the honey in a medium saucepan and bring to a seethe. Reduce the heat and simmer 5 mins till thickened sgently. Take away from the heat and add within the vanilla. Rain the syrup over the

warm baklava and allow soak for 2 hour or overnight. Enjoy!

Cheesy hasselback potato

prep time 15 mins
prepare time one hour
total time one hour 15 mins
<u>servings 6</u>

INGREDIENTS
- 3 pounds' baby potatoes, I like employing a medium size
- 2 tablespoons extra virgin olive oil
- 2 cups heavy cream or whole milk
- 2 cloves garlic, minced or grated
- half cup grated manchego cheese
- half cup grated gruyere cheese
- 1 tablespoon chopped fresh thyme
- 2 tablespoons butter, thinly sliced
- kosher salt and pepper

INSTRUCTIONS
1. 1. Preheat the oven to 425 degrees F.
- **Attentively slice the potatoes into thin slices, leaving a 1/8 inch at the bottom, be careful not to slice all the way**

through the potato. Place in a 9x13 inch baking dish and gently blend with olive oil, salt, and pepper. Place to the oven and roast for 20-25 mins.
- Meanwhereas, in a medium bowl, mix the cream, garlic, cheese, thyme, and a pinch every of salt and pepper.
- Take away the potatoes from the oven and Rain the cream over them, lay the potatoes in a mostly even layer. Place the slices of butter around the potatoes. Comeback to the oven and roast for another 20-25 mins, till the sauce thickens and the potatoes are tender. Spice with flaky salt simply before serving. Enjoy!

Roasted lemon spinach

prep time 15 mins
prepare time 30 mins
total time 45 mins
servings 8

INGREDIENTS
- 1 small, Meyer lemon
- 1 jalapeño, halved

- 2 cloves garlic
- 2 tablespoons extra virgin olive oil
- kosher salt and pepper
- 1 package (8 ounces) cream cheese, softened to about 25 °C
- one cup cubed fontina cheese
- one cup cubed mozzarella cheese
- half teaspoon smoked paprika
- 1 bag (ten ounces) frozen chopped spinach thawed drained and squeezed dry
- 1 jar (12 ounces) marinated artichokes, roughly chopped
- 2 tablespoons raw pine nuts
- fresh dill, for topping

INSTRUCTIONS

1. 1. Preheat the oven 375 degrees F.
- Slice one-third of the lemon into thin slices and put aside. Quarter the remaining lemon and take away the seeds.
- In a small baking dish, mix the quartered lemon, jalapeño, garlic, olive oil, and a pinch every of salt and pepper. Place to the oven and roast for 15-20 mins or till the lemon is golden and caramelized. Take away and allow cool. If desired, de-seed the jalapeño. Delicately chop the lemon, jalapeño, and garlic into a rough paste.
- In a medium bowl, mix the cream cheese, fontina, half of the mozzarella, the paprika, spinach, and artichokes. Add within the the roasted lemon paste. Spice to try with salt and pepper. Place to an 8-inch lubricated baking dish. Over with the remaining mozzarella and remaining lemon slices. Place to the oven and bake for 15-20 mins or till the cheese is melted. Submit warm, topped with pine nuts. Submit with fresh bread or crackers. Enjoy!

Cheese-maker mac and cheese

prep time 15 mins
prepare time 45 mins
total time one hour
servings 8

INGREDIENTS
- 7 tablespoons unsalted butter
- ¼ cup all-purpose flour
- 3 cups 2% or whole milk
- 1 pound elbow macaroni
- 1 garlic clove, minced or grated
- 1½ cups crushed Ritz Crackers (about 1 sleeve)
- 4 ounces' cream cheese, cut into cubes
- 1¼ cups shredded sharp white cheddar cheese
- 1¼ cups shredded fontina cheese
- one cup shredded Havarti cheese
- one cup shredded smoked Gouda cheese
- ¼ teaspoon cayenne
- Kosher salt and freshly ground pepper
- Fresh basil leaves, for topping

INSTRUCTIONS

1. 1. Preheat the oven to 350°F. Spatter a 9 x 13-inch baking dish with cooking spray.
- In a big saucepan, soften 4 tablespoons of the butter over medium heat. Blend within the flour. Reduce the heat to medium-low and prepare for 1 minute, stirring once to avoid burning—it can bubble. Gradually blend within the milk and 2 cups of water, then add within the macaroni. Increase the heat to medium-high and bring the mixture to a seethe. Add frequently till the macaroni is simply al dente, 8 to ten mins.
- Meanwhereas, in a medium skillet, soften the remaining 3 tablespoons of butter over medium-low heat. Place the garlic and prepare for 30 seconds, or till fragrant. Place the crushed crackers and blend to coat. Toast the crumbs till browned, stirring frequently to avoid burning, for 3 to 5 mins. Take away the pan from the heat and put aside.
- Just as the macaroni is al dente, take away the pan from the heat and add within the cream cheese, cheddar, fontina, Havarti, Gouda, and cayenne and spice with salt and pepper. Add till the cheeses have fully melted. Place the mixture to the pre readyd baking dish.
- Evenly strew the toasted cracker crumbs over the mac and cheese and place the baking dish on a baking sheet. Bake for 15 to 20 mins, or till the crumbs are golden brown and the sauce is bubbling. Take away from the oven and allow sit for 5 mins (yeah, right). Garnish with fresh basil. Dig in!

Cinnamon spiced dutch with cranberry butter

prep time ten mins
prepare time 20 mins
total time 30 mins
<u>servings 6</u>

INGREDIENTS
- 4 eggs
- 2/3 cup whole milk
- 2/3 cup Bob's Red Mill All-Purpose Flour
- 2 teaspoons vanilla extract
- 1 tablespoon hazelnut liquor (optional)
- 1 half teaspoons ground cinnamon
- One-quarter teaspoon freshly ground nutmeg
- half teaspoon kosher salt
- 4 tablespoons butter
- whipped cream and maple syrup, for serving

CRANBERRY BUTTER
- 4 tablespoons salted butter, at about 25 °C
- One-quarter cup leftover cranberry sauce

INSTRUCTIONS

1. 1. Preheat the oven to 450 degrees F. Place 2 tablespoons butter in a ten-12 inch cast iron skilallow and place the skilallow within the center of the oven.
- Whereas the skilallow is heating, in a blender, mix the eggs, milk, flour, vanilla, hazelnut liquor, if using, cinnamon, nutmeg salt, and 2 tablespoons liquified butter. Blend on high for 30 seconds to one minute or till the batter is sleek. Prepare sure no big clumps of flour remain. Take away the hot skilallow from the oven and Rain the batter into the skillet. Place the skilallow within the center of the oven and bake for 20-25 mins or till the pancake is fully puffed and browned on top. DO NOT open the oven during the first 15 mins of cooking or you might deflate your pancake.
- Meanwhereas, prepare the cranberry butter. In a medium bowl, blend along the butter and cranberry sauce till mixd.
- Take away the Dutch Baby from the oven and over with cranberry butter, allow it to melt. Then place whipped cream and maple. EAT.

Cheddar apple butternut squash soup

prep time 20 mins
prepare time 40 mins
total time one hour
servings 6

INGREDIENTS
- 3 tablespoons extra virgin olive oil
- 1 yellow onion, chopped
- 2 honeycrisp apples
- kosher salt and pepper
- One-quarter cup all-purpose flour
- 4 cups low sodium vegetable broth
- 4 cups cubed butternut squash
- half teaspoon cayenne pepper, more or less to taste
- one cup whole milk
- 1-2 cups shredded sharp cheddar cheese, depending on your taste
- 2 tablespoons + 2 teaspoons fresh thyme leaves

- 2 tablespoons salted butter
- 1 tablespoon honey

CINNAMON PECAN CRUMBLE
- 1 half cups raw pecans, roughly chopped
- one cup old fashioned oats
- 2 tablespoons all-purpose flour
- 2 tablespoons real maple syrup
- 1 teaspoon cinnamon
- 4 tablespoons salted butter, at about 25 °C

INSTRUCTIONS

1. 1. Heat the olive oil in a big pot over medium heat. Just as the oil shimmers, place the onion and 1 chopped apple. Prepare till fragrant, about ten mins. Blend within the flour and prepare till golden, about 2 mins, then gradually blend within the broth till sleek. Place the butternut squash, cayenne, and a big pinch every of salt and pepper. Bring to a seethe, reduce the heat to medium and cook, covered, till the squash is tender, about 20 mins.
- Take away the soup from the stove. Allow cool sgently and then puree in a blender or employ an immersion blender.
- Comeback the soup to the stove and set over low heat. Add within the milk and cheese till liquified and creamy. Place the thyme and prepare another 2-3 mins. Try and adsimply seasonings as desired.
- To prepare the honey butter apples. Soften the butter in a medium skilallow over medium-high heat. Place 1 thinly sliced apple and prepare till it simply begins to caramelize, about 5 mins. Place the honey and 2 teaspoons thyme. Prepare another minute, then take away from the heat.
- To service, ladle the soup into bowls and spoon the apples over top. Finish with a strew of pecan crumble. Enjoy!

CINNAMON PECAN CRUMBLE
1. 1. Preheat the oven to 350 degrees F.

- On a rimmed baking sheet, mix the oats, pecans, flour, maple, cinnamon, and a pinch of salt. Place the butter and employ your fingers to crumble it into the blend till everything is moist.
- Place to the oven and bake for 20 mins, stirring halfway through cooking, till crisp and golden brown and smells amazing. I like to submit this warm, so I prepare it whereas the soup simmers.

Butternut squash cheese ravioli

prep time 30 mins
prepare time 45 mins
total time one hour 15 mins
servings 8

INGREDIENTS
- 4 cups cubed butternut squash (about 1 medium squash)
- 1 tablespoon extra virgin olive oil
- kosher salt and pepper

- one cup whole milk ricotta cheese
- half cup crumbled gorgonzola cheese (may also employ goat cheese)
- half cup grated parmesan cheese
- 1 teaspoon honey
- 1 pound fresh pasta dough (or 40 wonton wrappers)

BROWNED BUTTER SAGE PESTO
- 4 tablespoons salted butter
- half cup fresh sage leaves, chopped
- 2 tablespoons extra virgin olive oil
- one cup Tuscan kale, delicately chopped
- One-quarter cup toasted pumpkin seeds, delicately chopped
- 2 tablespoons grated parmesan cheese
- kosher salt and crushed red pepper flakes

INSTRUCTIONS

1. 1. To prepare the ravioli. Heat up oven to 400 degrees F. On a baking sheet, blend along the butternut squash, olive oil, and a pinch every of salt and pepper. Place to the oven and roast for 25-30 mins or till the squash is tender.
- Place the squash to a food processor and place the ricotta, gorgonzola, parmesan, and honey. Puree till sleek. Spice with salt and pepper.
- Roll your pasta dough into lasagna sheets. Place 1 tablespoon of filling one inch apart over half the pasta sheet. Brush around the filling with water to moisten and then fold the sheet over the fillings, Puting down to seal. Cut into squares. Be sure to keep the ravioli covered as you work to prevent them from drying out. Recur with remaining dough and filling. Alternately, you'll prepare the ravioli in a ravioli Put.
- To prepare the pesto. In a big skillet, brown the butter over medium heat, stirring often till the butter is golden and toasted. Place the sage and prepare another minute.

Remove from heat, place the olive oil, kale, pumpkin seeds, parmesan, and spice to try with salt and crushed red pepper flakes.
- Bring a big pot of salted water to a seethe. Seethe the ravioli in batches about 1-2 mins or till they float. Drain.
- Share the ravioli among bowls and spoon the pesto over top. EAT and ENJOY!

6 ingredient spiced pumpkin butter

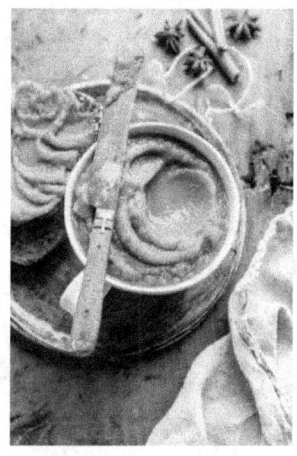

prep time ten mins
prepare time 20 mins
total time 30 mins
servings 32

INGREDIENTS
- 2 cans (15 ounce) pumpkin puree
- one-third cup apple cider
- half cup real maple syrup, plus more if needed to sweeten
- 1 tablespoon vanilla extract

- 1 tablespoon pumpkin pie spice
- 1 teaspoon cinnamon
- half teaspoon kosher salt

INSTRUCTIONS

STOVE-TOP

1. 1. In a medium sauce pan, mix the pumpkin, cider, maple syrup, vanilla, pumpkin pie spice, cinnamon, and salt. Bring to a gentle seethe over medium heat. Cook, stirring often till the pumpkin thickens sgently, however is unfoldable, about 20-30 mins. Taste, adding more maple syrup if needed to sweeten.
- Take away from the heat and allow cool (the pumpkin butter can thicken as it cools). Place to glass jars and keep stored within the fridge for up to 1 month or in freezer safe containers for up to 3 months.

SLOW COOKER

1. 1. Within the bowl of your slow cooker, mix the pumpkin, cider, maple syrup, vanilla, pumpkin pie spice, cinnamon, and salt. Overlay and prepare on high for 3-4 hours. During the last 45 mins of cooking, take away the lid to allow the pumpkin butter to thicken. Taste, adding more maple syrup if needed to sweeten.
- Put off the heat and allow cool (the pumpkin butter can thicken as it cools). Place to glass jars and keep stored within the fridge for up to 1 month or in freezer safe containers for up to 3 months.

Potato rolls

prep time 20 mins
prepare time 25 mins
servings 12

INGREDIENTS
- three-quarters cup warm water
- 2 half teaspoons instant yeast
- 2 tablespoons honey
- 2 big eggs
- one cup plain mashed potatoes*
- 3 cups all-purpose flour
- 1 half cups white whole wheat or whole wheat flour
- 1 teaspoon kosher salt
- 6 tablespoons salted butter, liquified + 2 tablespoons for brushing
- 1 tablespoon chopped fresh rosemary
- flaky sea salt, for topping

INSTRUCTIONS
1. 1. Within the bowl of a stand mixer, mix the water, yeast, honey, eggs, potatoes, flour, whole wheat flour, salt, and

- butter. Employing the dough hook, blend till the flour is completely incorporated, about 4-5 mins.
- Overlay the bowl with plastic wrap and allow sit at about 25 °C for one hour or till doubled in size.
- Lubricate a 9x13 inch baking dish with butter.
- Punch the dough down and share into 12 equal size dough balls. Lay within the pre readyd baking dish. Overlay the pan, and allow the rolls rise for about 30-45 mins, till they're puffy. Alternately, you'll place the pan within the fridge to rise overnight.
- Preheat the oven to 350. Bake the rolls for 20 to 25 mins, till they're golden brown on top.
- Meanwhereas, soften along the remaining 2 tablespoons butter and the rosemary till the butter is gently browned.
- Take away the rolls from the oven, and brush with the liquified rosemary butter, strew with salt, if desired. Pull them apart to submit warm.

RECIPE NOTES

*to prepare one cup of mashed potatoes, seethe 2 cups of peeled, cubed potatoes till fork tender, about 20 mins. Drain and mash.

Calories based on one serving size

Bourbon casserole

prep time 30 mins
prepare time one hour 40 mins
total time two hours ten mins
>   servings 8

INGREDIENTS

- 4 medium sweet potatoes
- 3 tablespoons real maple syrup
- 2 tablespoons bourbon (optional)
- 2 teaspoons vanilla extract
- 1 half teaspoons ground cinnamon
- One-quarter cup whole milk or cream
- 6 tablespoons salted butter, melted
- 2 eggs, gently beaten
- 12-18 sheets frozen phyllo dough, thawed

PECANS

- 2 tablespoons all-purpose flour
- 1 tablespoon real maple syrup

- one cup raw pecans, delicately chopped
- 1 tablespoon fresh chopped sage
- 2 tablespoons cold butter, cubed

INSTRUCTIONS

1. Preheat your oven to 400 degrees F. Butter an 8-9-inch spring form pan.

- Poke a few holes within the sweet potatoes and bake for one hour or till soft and tender. Just as the sweet potatoes are cooked, slice them in half and allow to cool down. Reduce the oven temperature to 350 degrees F.
- Peel the skins away from the sweet potatoes and mash well in a big mixing bowl. Blend within the maple syrup, bourbon (if using), vanilla, 1 teaspoon cinnamon, milk, 2 tablespoons butter, and eggs, mixing till mixd. Put aside whereas you pre ready the phyllo dough.
- In a small bowl, blend the remaining 4 tablespoons butter and half teaspoon cinnamon.
- Place 1 sheet of phyllo dough on a clean counter and brush with the cinnamon butter. Repeat, layering 2 more times, placing the sheets of dough over over of every other. Attentively Place the buttered phyllo to the pre readyd pan, gently Puting it to fit inside. Repeat, over lapping every layer 3 more times till you have completely covered the bottom and sides of the pan to Make the crust (see above photo) and have employd between 12-18 sheets of dough.
- Spoon the sweet potato mixture into center of the phyllo dough. Deploy in an even layer.
- To prepare the pecans. In a medium bowl, mix the flour, maple, pecans, and sage. Place the butter and employ your fingers to blend the butter into the pecans till a crumble forms.
- Strew the pecans over the sweet potatoes. Place to the oven and bake for 30-40 mins or till the pecans are toasted and the phyllo is golden brown. Submit warm

www.ingramcontent.com/pod-product-compliance
Lightning Source LLC
Chambersburg PA
CBHW072009070526
44583CB00015B/1397